RESPONSE TELEVISION

RESPONSE TELEVISION

Combat Advertising of the 1980s

John Witek

CRAIN
BOOKS

Published by Crain Books
A Division of Crain Communications, Inc.
740 Rush Street
Chicago, IL 60611

81 82 83 10 9 8 7 6 5 4 3 2 1

ISBN 0-87251-064-6
Library of Congress Catalog Card Number 81-66514

Printed in the United States of America

To Debbie Novak whose direct responses helped me to write this book.

"TV is above all a medium that demands a creative participant response."

Contents

Foreword

Response Television is a book that has been needed for years. It is needed more than ever today.

Television advertising is the most difficult advertising medium to measure. Some advertisers admit they cannot measure sales results at all. Others use nebulous measurements such as recall, telephone calls, etc.

John Witek has done a superb job in this book. It will be of great help to direct response advertisers. General advertisers will also find it valuable because it tells how to make TV commercials sell better. Students of advertising should make it must reading.

John Caples

Acknowledgments

For their help, encouragement and good advice the author is indebted to: Marilyn Arronson, Robert D. Burgener, Harold Bolling, Karen Burns, John Caples, Dom Cerulli, the Direct Mail/Marketing Association, Nancy Ann Donahue, Andi Emerson, Michael Fabian, Guy F. Gravenson, William Gregory, Gordon W. Grossman, Kathleen Hartnett, Sheldon Hechtman, Sheila James, Jim Kobs, George Lynaugh, Malcolm D. Kriger, Sy Levy, Paul A. Melnick, Jennifer Menten, Carol Milam, Francine Nyari, Betsy Proudfit (Advertising Research Foundation), Daniel Rubin, Richard L. Rubin, Kathryn Sederberg, Marlys Sherman, Stratis Simon, Robert Simpson, Emily Soell, Paul Stewart, Mike Slosberg, and George Wiedemann.

Special thanks to Joni K. Miller, Andi Mayer, and Debbie Novak for help in preparing this manuscript.

Introduction

"Mail order always does well in hard times."
—*Anonymous direct marketing adage*

In the coming age of interactive television when direct response advertising will be the principal form of advertising worldwide, the tremendous range of TV viewers' options in the home will contrast ironically to their shrinking options outside the home.

The family's video communications complex will bring almost everything, everywhere, into the home instantly. Developments that link computers and television will give us access to information and entertainment originating from all parts of the world. The same technology will allow us to conduct personal business directly through the television set, which will be able to send as well as to receive data. The range of imminent video communications will be so vast that television will serve us as teacher, jester, accountant, nursemaid, secretary, errand boy, paramedic, librarian, fire warden, and security guard.

Unlike the expanded range of video services, the scope of our lives will narrow. We'll travel less. Our money will buy less while our taxes will increase. Crime, the deteriorating environment, and a diminishing supply of energy will threaten our security. The shift from urban to suburban living will insulate us, possibly reducing our cultural vitality.

Hence the irony. Television in the closing decades of the twentieth century will do more and bring us more of everything. But it will do so during a time of profound anxiety.

It is necessary to keep in mind the irony of this predicament because, in part, the purpose of this book is to anticipate the conditions that will affect consumer behavior in order to help prepare direct response television for what it might confront. The way people are likely to react to hard times will help determine how products and services can be sold through television in the future—a future in which customers place their orders by talking directly into their television sets.

I hope readers will understand that I am not raising theoretical concerns for the sake of speculation. Advertising—direct response advertising in particular—is practical and rarely conjectural. The guesswork in this book is included to stimulate new work in advertising and lead to powerful new commercials such as we have never seen before.

But for direct response television advertising to grow, it needs ideas to push against. Until recently it has been by itself in a corner and hasn't encouraged nearly enough of the kind of discussion that nourishes a discipline. The theoretical aspect of this book is intended to provoke discussion. But bear in mind that the technology from which many of the projections stem already exists, often in applied form. So while we're looking up at the blue sky, we haven't forgotten where our feet are planted.

Readers are encouraged to disagree. The energy generated will be well worth the differences of opinion. It will be the kind of energy that enlivens direct response advertising and contributes to its growth and to its ultimate overtaking of traditional consumer advertising in scope, impact, and significance.

All things considered, it is foreseeable that today's large consumer advertising agencies will become dinosaurs— ineffectual relics of the past—if they do not acquire the response-producing capabilities that some of them are already pursuing and developing.

Future Direct Response Consumers

With that in mind, let's jump ahead a decade and consider the typical family that direct response TV advertising will serve—a white, middle-class married couple in their thirties with two school-age children. Most likely they will be living in a modern suburb of one of the increasingly popular Sunbelt states, for this will be a time when the upwardly mobile populations of eastern cities like New York, Boston, and Philadelphia will be lost to the Sunbelt in increasing numbers. The wife will work, as will the majority of American women. A consequence of this will be a decided shift away from women's traditional weekday shopping patterns.

In the light of these developments, it will become increasingly important for goods and services to find their way directly into the homes of consumers who will want things to come to them, instead of the other way around. Convenience has always been the principal reason for buying via direct response. The 1980s and '90s will be an age of convenience shopping.

The new focus of the home will be the family's video communications complex—the room housing the hardware that receives and transmits electronic data. Some of that hardware might be in the form of a massive wall screen, a future development of today's 84-inch giant screen projection systems. It will be cable-equipped and interactive, permitting the family not only to receive signals but also to send them. Cable television's two-way capability plus electronic funds transfer will make it possible to shop and bank at home. Two-way television will also be able to be programmed to link with private local protection services in order to serve as a fire and burglar alarm. The same system will fulfill educational needs—from preschool to graduate levels.

The interactive system that serves, protects, and educates will also entertain. As it was during the Depression of the 1930s when movies and radio programs were a welcome diversion from hard times, entertainment in the stressful and pessimistic 1980s will be a vital commodity. Cable television will make hundreds of channels available. Homemade videotapes will transform the TV screen into the family album. Video disks that can be played like records will add the dimension of sight to anything that previously could be only read or heard. Video games, from tic-tac-toe for tots to live casino gambling, could prove popular. And the most remarkable aspect of all the new entertainment will be the participatory dimension of television.

Viewers will actually be able to affect the course and outcome of the programs they watch by pushing the right buttons or by speaking directly into their television sets. They will be able to feed signals straight to broadcasters' central computers, allowing them to register their moves in a video game, select a happy instead of a tragic ending for a television movie, and perhaps even create the movie they are watching by registering their preferences through the viewer input control, twisting the plot and action as they see fit. Furthermore, two or more programs will be available for simultaneous viewing on the same screen—a made-for-pay-cable movie, for instance, and mortised into the upper right-hand corner of the screen, a football game or the news.

Choice and participation as never before will characterize family viewing. Viewers will be able to do something about what they watch, interact with it, shape it, and accept or reject it while it is happening.

This new, active relationship between viewer and video will

determine what will be the predominant mode of television advertising. It can only be direct response television advertising.

Laying the Groundwork

Advertising will be needed, as always, to make broadcasting profitable and to hold down the cost of video hardware for the home. And because the relationship of viewers to their televisions will become increasingly personal and active, we can assume that genuine *involvement* will also characterize television advertising. The kind of advertising encouraged by the new nature of television will be response advertising—the most vital and on-target advertising of the interactive age. Consumer advertising that requires a passive audience will be out of synch with the new mode of television and will seem as naive as some response advertising does today.

The form and content of television's new response advertising will be discussed later. Of interest here is how today's response specialists are laying the groundwork for the supremacy of response. Direct response professionals differ from other advertising people because their advertising is measurable. Reputations in the field of direct response have everything to do with precisely how many sales a commercial makes. Response specialists are totally accountable for the results of their efforts, and they operate with the authority of having made specific numbers of sales as well as images.

Understandably, marketers have often had a stronger influence than creative personnel on how direct response advertising looks. When you win or lose on nothing other than the number of orders pulled—and those results are immediate—it can seem more prudent simply to display and describe a product as marketers are likely to do, rather than take chances on a creative approach. Consequently, creative response advertising was squelched for many years by cautious direct marketers who contended that merely stating an offer was enough to make sales and who overlooked that it may well be the creativity of commercials that motivates viewers to act.

In addition to a bias against creative response advertising (*creative* meaning commercials that are every bit as imaginative as the best general advertising), the production of good response commercials was undercut by severely modest production budgets. During the 1960s and for much of the 1970s, $1,500 to $3,000 was considered just about what was worth spending on a direct response commercial. Salaries for creative personnel were also considerably lower than what the rest of the industry generally enjoyed. With little money for production or salaries, top creative talent shied away from response. Often the people who come to response from general advertising did so because they had reached the end of the trail on Madison Avenue and found that response operations could be convenient places to hide away.

It's not hard to understand why major consumer accounts failed to see response as being of service to them until the mid-1970s. By then a creative momentum had been set in motion based on the hard-won successes of advertisers who were bold enough to deviate from response clichés and who pumped life into their advertising with ideas and approaches drawn largely from general advertising. By the end of the 1970s, television response advertising had proved itself capable of being fresh, exciting, effective, and valuable to a widening circle of clients.

The annual sales of products and services marketed directly was approaching $100 billion in 1979. The 1981 *Direct Marketing Fact Book* charts direct response television expenditures in 1979 at $212 million and skyrocketing. As this phenomenal growth continues, the bastard child of the advertising industry may stand up and cast a shadow that could eclipse consumer advertising's place in the sun. Cars, furniture, jewelry, alcoholic beverages, food, clothing, necessities, and luxuries are all likely to find their way into the home through direct response commercials that are both the sales message and the salesperson. Response specialists have spent years learning how to close a deal or parlay it into a better deal. General agencies have never even addressed the problem.

Lester Wunderman, founder of one of the world's leading direct response agencies, Wunderman, Ricotta & Kline, outlined some of the reasons for the response industry's growth in a speech to the agency in March 1979.

> The industry will grow because direct marketing's time has come. Employed families—that is, families in which the husband and wife both work—are beginning to dominate the middle and upper income groups. These families have less time for shopping—and want more convenience and more service. Direct marketing is becoming a better, faster, easier way to shop.
>
> Inflation and the increasing cost of goods and people continue to eat into the margins of conventional retailers. They have less to spend on service—and there is no technology in sight which can help them, except a change

in the idea of retailing itself. The new technologies are all on our side. Touch-tone telephones placing orders directly into computers—satellite television available on cable with fewer restrictions on the length of commercials—interactive television—telephone selling—automated warehouses—all are existing technologies ready now! They are not future dreams. They are already in the marketplace. Our clients know this, and more and more companies will discover it every day.

The growing scarcity and high prices of gasoline will make many shopping trips uneconomic or even impossible. If people can't or won't go to the merchandise, then the merchandise will have to go to them. The home will become the shopping center of the future. Direct marketing, as we will practice it, will replace that part of the distribution system which is too expensive, too inconvenient, or already obsolete.

The direct marketing industry is already growing faster than any other distribution method here and abroad.

Consumer Behavior Changes

Wunderman's emphasis on new consumer needs and values touches upon broad changes in American behavior, attitudes, and shopping preferences that will color the 1980s. Modern consumer behavior will not be the comfortable expression of an optimistic people harvesting the fruit of the American dream that it was in the 1940s, '50s, and '60s when the foundation for the style of today's consumer advertising was laid. Instead, marketers will be faced with Americans who are becoming increasingly isolated from the traditional marketplace—both physically and temperamentally—as well as from the social, political, and intellectual life of the nation.

As inflation and the recession worsen, we don't know whether to hold on to our money or to spend it. The homogenization of goods and services that makes one product much like another has taken the zest out of over-the-counter shopping, resulting in fewer bargains, surprises, and real differences. Shopping around seems less and less profitable. You only find the same goods in different places and end up wasting time and gas to boot. If you live in the city, especially if you're elderly, a shopping trip can set you up for a mugging or a purse snatching.

A consequence of consumer dissatisfaction is the economic confusion of the individual. This runs contrary to the national tendency of buying as a way of life. An American is one who buys, and the free exercise of our purchasing power has been encouraged for decades as a way of proving our freedom and independence to ourselves and to one another. But now, reacting to an atmosphere of national and personal impoverishment, we tend to buy schizophrenically. We buy less. We buy cautiously, on the lookout for economy, value, durability, with no frills and no frivolity.

Or we go the other way. We splurge, sopping up luxuries, the top of the line, things we feel we may not be able to afford next year—or next month, for that matter. We go after the good life now, because tomorrow the stereo we want is going to be twice as expensive. Or our money will become as worthless as so many inflated reichsmarks. Or gas supplies will run out. Or the nuclear reactor will leak. Or the bomb will drop. Or who knows what, and we're scared as hell. And so we've wrapped our fears in layers of skepticism, cynicism, and inertia. Booze and drugs stave off reality. So does television, which is a background presence in most homes, like a child's night-light—familiar, comforting, yet not particularly attention-getting.

Hard hit as we are by these times and insulated against them, we sit passively in front of our television sets waiting for the next shock wave. Curiously, this passive mode of behavior is important to direct response advertising's potential to become the most effective kind of television advertising.

Direct Response—The Active Option

In order to sell, response advertising has to convert viewers from passivity and disinterest to active participation. It must engage the imagination to produce simple behavior shifts, such as getting up from a chair to dial a telephone. Direct response aims for positive action. And people feel good about positive action because acting gives the impression of being in control. Thus the act of buying through direct response television is accompanied by positive associations that do not accompany general consumer advertising.

The slickest, costliest general agency productions cannot make a prospective customer get up and do something *now*. Consumer advertising seeks to leave its audience with a simple impression that influences their behavior at some time in the future. But direct response advertising works immediately. It takes customers by the hand and leads them every step of the way up to and through the sales transaction. Our commercial has to involve viewers the moment they experience it. Our dynamics are different. Our timing is different. We manipulate more details. We try to anticipate consumer reservations in order to find out how to produce positive action and make sales. We are the whole show, embracing the message and the means of ordering. Being what we are, direct response fulfills the promise of a direct link between buyer and seller that television has always implied.

The history of television contains one example after another of viewers' willingness to participate in what they are watching. When a telethon host asks for contributions or a children's program character asks youngsters to spell along with the picture on the screen, the results are affirmative. Viewers do what they are asked to do if they are approached in the right way. Response advertising, like the participatory aspect of television, is intensely personal. And working on such a personal level, it is the kind of advertising that is met with an extra long, hard look by consumers. The only advertising that can stand up under such scrutiny is advertising that engages the heart and mind and literally *moves* the viewer to order.

This positive action is self-reinforcing. The act of ordering resonates with feelings of self-reliance, strength, and independence. By buying direct, customers can feel that they are shaping a small piece of their own future, a comforting feeling when times are as tough as they are today. This is one of the reasons for the old direct marketing adage that direct response always does well in hard times. Customers perceive direct response commercials as being helpful to them because the commercials make it possible for them to do something for themselves—now, not tomorrow at the supermarket, dealership, or appliance store but now, at home, over the telephone.

Of all advertising, only response has the *now*. And the many great nows of the future are what this book anticipates.

I've called direct television response advertising *combat advertising* because it has the toughest job to do—make immediate sales. It has developed a formidable arsenal of techniques and resources to accomplish that frontline objective repeatedly, effectively, and cost-efficiently. That arsenal will help us get in close to engage our segmented target audiences and break through the lethargy that generally affects American consumers. Nothing less than the methods and techniques of direct response advertising will combat the negativism and depression that accompany hard times.

Television response advertising pursues its objectives aggressively and without compromise. This is not to say that commercials of the future will be marked by the crude, shrill hawking that typifies many current low-budget response spots.

Quite the contrary. The more we test to determine the precise effects of direct response imagery and rhetoric, the more sophisticated our commercials will become. The marketing and strategies will be patently aggressive, but the executions will be varied, innovative, and on target.

Until now we have seen only a handful of commercials that prefigure the coming revolution in response advertising. These are commercials that can be judged creative by all current standards for quality advertising, and it is creativity that will spearhead the direct response revolution on television. In this book I hope to stimulate the creativity that will illuminate the future of advertising. That future *is* direct response.

This book focuses on television. It emphasizes the thinking behind direct response commercials and the ways of creating better response commercials that appeal to an ever-widening audience. It places its ideas within a tradition known as mail order and argues for ways to extend that tradition during the years to come. I hope it will make those of us who work in direct response even prouder of our discipline, and those less acquainted with direct marketing more aware of the promise it holds.

—J.W.

1
History, Larceny, and Much, Much More

Direct marketing got started when Montgomery Ward & Company published the first mail-order catalog in 1872. It caught up with twentieth-century technology 74 years later, when the first direct response commercials were televised around 1946.

When television was still in the planning stages, many of its developers thought of it primarily as a marketing tool. After all, radio would always be there to inform and entertain. So it's not surprising that as soon as television had a real audience, pitchmen began using it to convince people to buy this, that, and the other thing in the comfort of their own homes.

TV pitchmen were cleaning up by the 1950s. They convinced people to buy products without touching them or asking questions about them or trying them out. Viewers were running on their faith in a bargain. Given the right direct response pitchman, like the ubiquitous Joel Holt, in-home shoppers would buy practically anything—storm windows, silverplate, dishware, and the famous mail-order encyclopedia that could tell the little girl in the commercial why the sky was blue. Only a handful of these unique salesmen were responsible for the best of the TV pitches.

The Magic of Momentum

The name of the game was, and still is, _momentum_—a flow of vivid rhetoric that sweeps viewers away on a tide of words and images. Momentum is not information, it is style; it is a way of presenting information that turns passive TV watchers into active, telephone-dialing, letter-writing customers.

One aspect of people ordering merchandise through television is the need to fill the vacuum left by a performance that engages their imaginations. Buying something can be an emo-

1

tional release like applauding at a concert or making a donation at church on Sunday. The old TV pitchmen acted like preachers at a revival meeting, and the audience, caught up in the momentum of words, ordered products, in part, to break the tension when the pitch was over. When a religious service reaches an emotional peak following the sermon, the collection plate is passed. Likewise, the "here's-how-to-order" part of a direct response commercial follows an emotionally charged demonstration.

Sliced Onions and Shredded Cabbage

Early direct response commercials were the B movies of the advertising industry. The camera angles were few and simple—a medium shot of the pitchman with the product and a close-up to demonstrate the product—but the spiels were relentless and hypnotic. And people responded enthusiastically.

Following is a verbatim transcript of a mid-1950s direct response commercial. The announcer never pauses to take a breath. His hands never stop demonstrating. Words pile on top of words the same way that sliced onions and shredded cabbage pile up on the screen. What's important is the cumulative impression; the overwhelming argument for the product based on the sheer weight of details is the important element.

If you could actually listen to this commercial, you would hear how the speed of the delivery alone could hold the audience. Like an evangelist who moves his congregation emotionally, the TV pitchman used a fast cadence of carefully chosen words to produce a similar effect. But instead of a collection plate, he used a telephone number. The sermon went like this:

> . . . I'm going to make you a present of one of my juice extractors. Insert it in a lemon, serve it on the table like a saltshaker! For iced tea, for fish, or for salad, it's wonderful. Present number two is our adjustable slicing machine, for slicing cucumbers for salad, slicing potatoes for potato chips. But best of all, when you can go home and shred down some cabbage for cole slaw and cabbage for salad, it all comes out like shredded wheat. Now the reason why we do this is in order to advertise and introduce the new Grate And Shred. This side is made for making your California health salad. This side is made for taking the place of the old tin can, and you'll never cut your fingers. Now imagine going home for grating down some coconut and cheese and chocolate—I want you to

know that it works like an electric machine. Best of all, for making the raw vegetable juices, underneath the grater you place a cheesecloth—doctors and dietitians from all parts of the world recommend carrot juice because it contains Vitamin A. And do you know that if you drink this two or three times a week, by golly, you'll put the doctors right out of business. Now you're all wondering what they sell for. During this special offer, the Grate And Shred is on sale for two dollars—if you order one today, I'm going to make you a present of my slicing machine. I'm also going to make you a present of my juice extractor. This is made for taking all of the juice from the fruit, and that's not all. As a special bonus, I'm going to include my automatic pancake turner. That's the one that's made especially for flipping over eggs and pancakes and flipjacks and flapjacks. In other words you get a four-dollar outfit, the entire four pieces for only two dollars. Stand by for that important phone number and address.

Despite the fractured grammar and syntax, it was a compelling performance with 430 words fired off in two minutes. That's about 50 more words per minute than most of today's response commercials can comfortably accommodate—quite an accomplishment, considering that direct marketers continually search for new ways to cram more information into their commercials. Currently, sophisticated and complex visuals communicate much of the information that direct response commercials have to get across. But I have no doubt that if the old Grate And Shred commercial ran today with the product selling for $9.95 instead of $2, it might still be a winner.

It's a great commercial. Exciting imagery keeps popping up to pique the viewer's imagination: the juice extractor that you put on the table "like a saltshaker," cabbage that comes out like "shredded wheat," and, of course, "California health salad—you'll never cut your fingers—works like an electric machine." The commercial even has an appealing aside about "putting the doctors right out of business."

The visuals are as fast-paced as the copy. Seeing is believing; everything that is said is done. The pitchman never stops slicing, grating, and juicing. We know Grate And Shred is a miracle machine because we see the miracle happen.

The pitchman pounded home his points relentlessly, and then he stacked the deck. One, two, *three* free gifts (or presents, as he called them) were yours for ordering promptly. In the trade we call them premiums, but whatever you call a gift, it usually spells orders. Hardly anyone can resist something for nothing, which is why premiums have continued to be a mainstay of direct response advertising in general. Even today's "free" examination is a first cousin to the something-for-nothing approach.

The word *free* speaks to the heart; and like the effect of a mesmerizing, rapid-fire pitch, an appeal to the emotions encourages people to act without thinking. Premiums work; and that can be good or bad. They boost response; they also boost your break-even cost. And like sweepstakes, it's hard to stop using premiums once you start. Use a premium once and you might find that your audience expects you to use one the next time you sell your product, and you might not want to do that, especially on television where the time spent mentioning a free gift might be spent more wisely on the product itself.

Boardwalk Pitchman

One of the first entrepreneurs to kick off the TV selling business was a man named Daniel Rubin, who began selling Florida Fashions direct on television in 1946. His contribution was the basis for much that has followed because he used television to bring the street-corner pitchman into the home. Rubin knew that when it came to selling, no one could top the fast operators who worked the boardwalk in Atlantic City and who knew how to squeeze a sucker better than anyone else. So Rubin hit the boardwalk with a tape recorder and went to work. He taped pitches in the field; he also invited pitchmen to his New York office where he would film their acts for simple direct response commercials.

The sales figures proved that Rubin was doing something right because his style permeated the industry. For decades to come, direct marketing companies used the same pitching format successfully.

More notable than Rubin is Alvin Eicoff of Chicago, a pioneer who is doing more commercials today than ever. His work dates back to 1947, and he is responsible for many of the industry's standards, including the two-minute direct response commercial. Another pioneer in the field is Suffolk Marketing's Malcolm Smith of Slim Whitman fame.

Most of the products sold through direct response television during the 1950s and '60s were products for the home—kitchen gadgets and appliances, art prints, tools, books, and records. What better way to sell products for the home than through television, the product that had become a focal point of most

American living rooms? Television could demonstrate what direct marketers had to offer, and demonstrations backed by a carnival-barker delivery proved irresistible to a large segment of television's growing audience.

Early direct response commercials were crude and effective. They were filmed unimaginatively, narrated at a nagging rapid-fire pace, and always ended with a telephone number and address—often the TV station's address to give viewers confidence that it was safe to order. Success followed success.

Winning commercials based on the pitch have never stopped coming. The only difference between the old spots and the new is that now there are a few more camera angles and tape is often used instead of film. Current pitches are good for a laugh if you're not in the market for a home exercising device or a gizmo that scrambles an egg in its own shell. But there's no laughing at the bottom line where you can see the proof that some of these low-budget commercials can move products like mad.

Most of these commercials look cheap, and one reason for this is that there are many more losers than winners in low-ticket, one-shot marketing. The underlying philosophy has been to put a lot of products on the air in the hope that the one that sells will make up for the nine that don't. Since little preliminary testing is done with products or creative executions and since low-budget TV direct marketing is usually just educated guesswork, one-shot operations are reluctant to spend money on TV commercial production. Thus, the "B-movie" look will probably be with response television for some time to come.

Celebrities

Celebrities began to pop up in direct response commercials in the early 1950s. Sportscaster Bill Stern, appearing for Popeil, was one of the first. Familiar announcers like Dennis James and Don Wilson sold fine art prints and classical recordings. In 1969 the Longines Symphonette Society caused quite a stir when singer Helen O'Connell appeared in commercials selling the company's big band era record treasuries. O'Connell's commercial actually brought her back to the public's attention, and the same has proved true for a number of other fading stars who have appeared in direct response commercials. Success is risky in one-shot direct marketing, but many stars continue to work for modest fees plus a percentage of sales.

Athletes, singers, and musicians are seen most often in direct response commercials and in commercials supporting direct response advertising. The following, though incomplete, will give you an idea of who has sold what.

George Steinbrenner	New York Telephone's Sportsphone
Lou Pinella	Sportsphone
Ed Kranepool	Sportsphone
Jerry Koosman	Sportsphone
John Mendenhall	Sportsphone
Too-Tall Jones	Tall Men's Fashion Catalog
Reggie Jackson	TV support for Olympic posters sold through New York Telephone's billing series
John Williams	Classical records
Mitch Miller	Sing-A-Long records
Kenny Rogers	Kenny Rogers Songbook
Glenn Ford	Academy Life Insurance
Robert Stack	Continental American Life Insurance
Liberace	Piano Book
Rudy Vallee	Big Band records
Tony Randall	Betty Crocker recipe cards
Dorothy Lamour	Bing Crosby records
Fabian	Rock and roll records
Eddie Mecca	Rock and roll records
Dick Clark	Columbia Record Club support
Señor Wences	RCA Record Club support
Roy Clark	Roy Clark Songbook
Buster Crabbe	TV Tummy Trimmer
Mike Douglas	Save the Children Federation
Perry Como	North Shore Animal League
Art Linkletter	Unity Buying Service

Although it will be a long time before Sophia Loren asks viewers to call a toll-free number, there is a definite upswing in the use of top talent in direct response and support advertising.

Show and Tell

The creative approach of direct response commercials that has worked well over the last four decades is summed up in the kindergarten phrase—show and tell. The camera shows what the announcer is talking about as he tells about it. If he says a knife can slice through a beer can, we see the knife cutting metal at the same time the claim is made. If we're told that burnt cheese won't stick to a frying pan's nonstick surface, we see the charred mess slide right out at the same time. If a TV record package contains 20 songs, we see the names of all 20 songs in superimposed titles that crawl up the screen as the announcer names them.

Words set the stage for something special to happen; they

must be there to support what is happening as it is happening. This is how a commercial tells the audience what it is seeing or should be seeing. If the audience sees what you want it to see, it is far more likely to do what you want it to do!

Show and tell works. It sells products. But now that direct marketers are using television more widely and ambitiously than ever, we have to ask: To whom are we showing what we're showing? And how are we going to show it and talk about it? What are we going to single out from all the choices we can make? Are the visuals and the soundtrack working together as well as they possibly can? Will our show and tell work better in some parts of the country than in others? Or with certain age groups? Or in particular time slots?

Behind all the questions is one main question. How can we get a commercial to perform like a gold-star salesperson who knows how to come out on top when facing a customer and who knows how to make each person in a crowd feel like he or she is the only person being addressed?

Good salespeople are keenly intuitive. Their game plans are buttoned down. They know how to make sales by tailoring their act to the person in front of them. They are masters of vocal inflection, eye contact, subtle aggression, suggestion, flattery, humor, confidentiality, snobbishness, conviviality—whatever the situation calls for. Direct response television at its best aims to translate these human skills into film and tape. This goal makes it the powerful sales tool it has become. In the combat advertising of the 1980s, we will be looking for more effective ways to turn face-to-face selling into TV copy and graphics. It is possible that the commercials coming out of this search will be so deep and personal that they will seem to *produce* behavior in the viewer.

Consumer Distrust

As promising as direct response television is, however, it has always been regarded with so much suspicion that millions of people who might become customers steer clear. Many early commercials were highly questionable, like the so-called *integrated* commercials produced by the Charles Antell Company in the late 1940s and early 1950s. These commercials masqueraded as legitimate programs and were 15 or 30 minutes long. They were written like the TV shows of the day but were nothing more than extended sales pitches for vitamins, food processors, beauty products, and hair preparations.

Subsequent Federal Communication Commission (FCC) rulings and the evolution of television into a structured format of 30-, 60-, and 90-minute shows eliminated program-length commercials. Nevertheless, much of the public's dissatisfaction with direct response advertising on television was not eliminated and has continued to the present.

Abuses were rife in the early buccaneering days. Products sold through television might arrive months after they were ordered, while others never arrived at all. A lot of the merchandise that did show up was third rate.

Some commercials were vicious come-ons for shark-toothed salesmen with shady real estate deals, phony freezer food plans, overpriced house siding, fake diet pills, and junk encyclopedias at premium prices. The principles of truth in advertising and a full disclosure of the terms of the sale were often disregarded. The TV audience was finding out the hard way that an offer that sounded too good to be true really was too good to be true.

As a result, viewers learned to watch direct response commercials defensively, looking out for the catch. That defensiveness has carried over to the present day. Small wonder, since today's straight-arrow direct response spokesmen have only recently evolved from the former TV pitchmen, many of whom learned their trade from crooked faith healers and con artists who worked carnivals and street corners.

Of course, consumer safeguards protect viewers to some extent today. Direct marketers can no longer advertise imaginary products to determine if there is enough consumer demand to make the manufacture of those products profitable. The Federal Trade Commission's (FTC's) "30-Day Delayed Delivery Rule" specifies that mail-order merchandise must be shipped within 30 days of receiving a valid order, unless the advertising clearly and conspicuously notes another clear-cut period of time when shipment will be made. Under the rule, which went into effect in 1976, buyers can cancel and get a refund for delayed delivery beyond the stated period.

Other FTC rules and guidelines cover negative option plans, guarantees, warranties, testimonials, endorsements, sweepstakes, and the use of the words "free" and "new." They also define deceptive advertising, deceptive pricing, and bait-and-switch advertising.

Nevertheless, every now and then you can still hear a trace of the snake-oil salesman in direct response commercials, and that trace harms the entire industry. It makes it harder to do business with the people who do not yet make direct response purchases—that is, the majority of American consumers.

Suspicion of direct response advertising is a problem that only time and business ethics can heal. Direct response advertisers must allay the public's fears before they can serve the public on the grand scale television implies.

Satire and Public Opinion

By the time the Federal Trade Commission's most important rules governing direct response advertising went into effect, a lot of negative opinion had accumulated. Television comedy is a barometer of public opinion, and it is revealing that almost as soon as response commercials went on the air, comedians began taking potshots at them.

Jackie Gleason is one well-known comic who fired a good shot in a November 1955 broadcast of "The Honeymooners." In that episode, Ralph Kramden's newest get-rich-quick scheme was to put on a chef's hat, get on television, and sell Handy Dandy Housewife Helpers—his version of Grate And Shred. But Ralph got stage fright and mangled his hand with his own miracle machine. Bellowing like a wounded bull, he thrashed around on camera, destroying the set and any credibility his product might have had. The skit hinged on the fact that Kramden wanted to make a fast buck. It is only one of many times that direct response advertising has been singled out as a fast-buck operation that people had better avoid.

More recently, "Saturday Night Live" has spoofed direct response commercials. Dan Ackroyd's "commercials" for Rumco satirize those by the Ronco Corporation—a direct response TV heavyweight whose net sales in 1979 totaled $30 million. At that time, Ronco was still using the old-fashioned, overblown style of pitching to sell all sorts of "miracle" products for the home. Ackroyd came on slicker and more fervently than the commericals he satirized. Yes, you could do practically anything with one of Ackroyd's products. "You can pick it up, put it down, push it across the table, bang it on the wall, rub it on your head—isn't that amazing!" In other words, big deal!

Bob and Ray also took a swing at direct response on "Saturday Night Live." Their target was the typical exercise device sold on television, which usually turns out to be a cheap piece of junk. It won't get rid of much fat, but it can slenderize your wallet.

In their takeoff of a then current response spot, Bob and Ray imitated the real commercial practically frame by frame. (No great feat since the tacky, unimaginative original probably cost only a few thousand dollars to produce in the first place.) They sold "the Amazing Home Jogger that lets you jog in the comfort and privacy of your own home, while the pounds just seem to melt away." When you finally got a look at the product, it turned out to be two pieces of cardboard stuck to someone's feet with rubber bands for jogging in place. A superimposed title informed the viewer: "Rubber bands not included."

Then there were spoofs of record offers. Records and tapes have been among the most widely advertised direct response products—and perfect targets for comedians. Robert Kline, David Steinberg, and Johnny Carson have all done versions of the "all the music ever recorded for only $1.98" joke, a caricature of the "lots-for-little" marketing strategy. Carson even offered a deluxe edition of all the music ever recorded *excluding* Jerry Vale records.

For the most part, comedians have singled out:

1. the cheap, tacky look of many response commercials
2. the inferior, misrepresented products they sell
3. the questionable, hyperbolic marketing techniques they employ

People laugh because they see truth in the comedy. And as long as they laugh, direct marketers who want to expand their markets and find new ones will have hard going.

Toward Quality

Assessing public opinion about direct response television is like watching a balancing act. Poor commercials (which, unfortunately, have been in the majority) depress the state of the art and encourage negative opinion. Good commercials, fair offers, and decent products have the opposite effect. The balancing act was particularly evident during the 1970s, which was an active decade for direct response TV advertisers. It began with a bit of luck, and that resulted in television being more widely used as a response medium than ever before.

In 1970, cigarette advertising was abruptly banned on television. Both networks and local stations suddenly had more time on their hands than they could live with. Scrambling to fill the holes in their schedules left by the lost cigarette commercials, stations sold time at substantial discounts. Canny direct marketers jumped at the chance to buy inexpensive time and quickly produced and ran a lot of cheap commercials. Several years later when the cost of time rose again, the *schlockmeisters* became less active.

An equation became evident: quality or lack of quality in direct response commercials depended greatly on the cost of the media used. Cheap-looking commercials generally ran on local stations during the inexpensive daytime and late night hours; better looking commercials (support commercials in particular) ran during the more costly prime-time hours. This is not to say that local late night television isn't profitable. It can be. But when and where direct response commercials run and how they look certainly influence general public opinion about this method of advertising. Television viewers are likely to judge a commercial with a toll-free 800 number by the *kind* of commercial it is and not by its own merits. Everything that detracts from response television as a whole probably affects the performance of individual commercials. Similarly, everything that helps to upgrade response television brings it closer to becoming the preeminent advertising medium.

Since the early 1970s, the industry has pushed to build more quality into direct response commercials. The more that direct marketers have used television, the better their commercials have become. And it all began with a single commercial supporting direct mail.

The Support Breakthrough

Television support is a response-related form of advertising developed by people who thought in terms of direct marketing. It's important to look closely at support advertising because it has spurred the growth and acceptance of all direct response advertising on television.

Support advertising tells you to look for some other kind of advertising that's coming your way. A typical support commercial says watch the mail or look in Sunday's paper for a special announcement calling for a direct response. Support is used by direct marketers to boost response rates by creating advance interest in any of several forms of direct response advertising— print ads, newspaper and magazine inserts, or direct mail packages.

Support advertising has been around for more than 25 years. The brainchild of George Perkins of Schwab, Beatty and Porter, among others, it was given the go-ahead by client Walter Weintz when he was circulation director for *Reader's Digest*. The first simple support commercial was tested in an obscure market for a few hundred dollars. It told viewers to watch the mail for a subscription offer from *Reader's Digest*. The test proved that support could increase response significantly. And support advertising has been with us ever since. Naturally, *Reader's Digest* ran many subsequent campaigns, but one *Digest* commercial in particular stands out as a milestone.

Produced around 1972, this commercial was good looking, powerful, and conceptually different. While telling viewers to look for a sweepstakes mailing, it showed efficient-looking women on stepladders who were pinpointing the hometowns of previous *Digest* sweepstakes winners on a huge map of the United States. As name after name of past winners were read in a voice-over, an on-camera announcer assured viewers that they, too, could win.

The commercial was remarkable because it looked as good as anything else on television. It looked as though it had been done by a classy agency—and it had. The 1972 *Reader's Digest* support commercial was conceived and executed by J. Walter Thompson Company and was one of the first response-related commercials by a major agency. The quality showed in every aspect of the production.

In this milestone commercial, style was as important as content. It was the first big commercial concerned with response advertising that looked as good as general advertising. It was shown on prime-time network television, which created an even greater parity between the two forms of advertising.

Thompson's commercial for the *Digest* looked good for one simple reason. They spent money on it. A well-heeled client with standards to maintain paid for quality and got it. Other prosperous advertisers, notably the magazine subscription agency Publishers Clearing House, along with Time Incorporated and Bell Telephone, followed suit with support and direct response commercials produced with enough money to meet or surpass the prevailing standards for quality advertising on television.

With this advance in quality through production dollars came new excursions into a variety of general advertising genres, such as documentary treatments, humorous vignettes, slice-of-life situations, and movie parodies. These treatments had never before really been brought off successfully in direct response commercials.

A Spur to Creative

Bigger budgets for distinguished clients spurred the creative side of response advertising. Since standards for quality were being established, it became harder for a reputable client to do anything second rate. The advent of quality response and support advertising was also a signal to the major mass marketers that response was something they need not be ashamed of. In fact, they discovered that response advertising was downright intriguing.

First, response advertising is accountable. You know exactly how many sales result from the dollars you spend on advertising. Second, you can fine-tune a TV response campaign very effectively by monitoring response rates daily. Moreover, direct response can use one commercial to make more than one sale. The club or continuity approach—with or without membership commitments —encourages customers to accept regular monthly installments of products. All this looked good to mass marketers like Procter & Gamble and General Foods who, in the 1970s, were finally starting to think that there just might be something to all the commercials telling viewers to watch the mail or call toll-free.

The Direct Response Difference

Direct response had come a long way from Grate And Shred. It's not surprising, then, that the 1970s saw the giant agencies courting and buying up smaller, successful independent response agencies or trying (and often failing) to start their own direct response operations. One thing was clear. Direct response people saw television differently than did the rest of Madison Avenue. A lot of that difference had to do with direct marketers' backgrounds in print and mail in which the tone of the advertising was more intimate and personal than general advertising.

A Personal Touch

In a large sense, a direct response commercial is more like a direct mail package than it is like an ordinary television commercial. Both direct mail and direct response television ask for an immediate decision from one person—and from one person alone.

The direct mail letter lets the copywriter assume a personality through which to talk directly to a single customer. The best letters always have the flavor of one person talking to another, similar to face-to-face selling between one salesperson and one customer. Direct mail can do this because it's specific. We know who we are talking to because we can make reasonable assumptions about the names on the mailing lists we use. Likewise, in response television, we know the sex, age, education, and income of our prospects in advance. We know what time of day or night they watch television. We know approximately how many of them are out there. We know how the seasons, even the months, affect their buying habits. And we know which programs will encourage or discourage their responsiveness to an offer.

A perfect example of an on-target commercial where the advertiser knew its audience is a prizewinning 60-second spot for International Correspondence Schools. The copywriter reasoned that the prospect (the viewer without a college degree) might understandably be anxious about his or her future and might be willing to take advice from a firm, uncompromising authority figure. What makes the commercial exceptional is the casting of the announcer as a tough, no-nonsense authoritarian who talks straight into the camera without blinking. A single close-up of the man's face occupies the entire 60 seconds. The inescapable impression is of one person talking to another.

> Look, you've talked yourself out of getting a college degree. And I know why: inflation, your full-time job, your family.
> But those reasons are just excuses— Because the Center for Degree Studies makes accredited college degrees possible for people in your situation. You don't have to *go* to school. Your home is your classroom.
> You study at your own pace in the career field you choose.
> And you're guided by a dedicated faculty that's always available, toll free, 12 hours a day. All you need is a high school diploma and the drive to get a degree.
> Call the number below for our free catalog. There's no obligation—the catalog explains everything. Wouldn't you rather make more of your life instead of just letting it slip away? © International Correspondence Schools

Direct response commercials talk to individuals. This is nothing like the mainstream TV commercials that seem to address a crowd. *We* are told to drink Dr Pepper or fly Pan Am (who flys the *world* the way the world wants to fly). Or come on, America, or hey there, New Yorkers, do X, Y, and Z. The fact is that *you* are not being asked to do any of these things. General advertising tends to talk to consumers in the aggregate; direct response talks to *you*. And it has to be that way because if *I* want *you* to get up and make a phone call, I had better be sure that I'm talking to *you* and not to a faceless crowd.

Similarities to Mail

In addition to their personal tone, direct response commercials have other elements that are similar to direct mail. The direct mail letter "tells" and the brochure "shows" just as the commercial tells and shows. A direct mail order card and a commercial's closing telephone number serve the same purpose.

Direct marketers have an ideal sequence of events in mind when they create direct mail packages. The outer envelope attracts your attention and gets you inside the package so you won't throw away the mailing. The letter does the heavy selling and urges you to buy something. The brochure shows you what it is. The order card, usually incorporating an action device, makes it easy for you to order.

Direct response commercials work in the same way but are more concentrated. The commercial is written to grab your attention in the first five seconds. Words and pictures work together as though a direct mail letter had been wedded to a brochure. The telephone number and address at the end of the commercial is an audio-visual order card; the only difference is you don't drop it in a mailbox, you pick up the telephone and dial.

There is one more parallel between response mail and response television. A few years ago, Wunderman, Ricotta & Kline came up with a gimmick called a transfer device to measure the effectiveness of TV support advertising. A small illustration is printed on the announcement the commercial is supporting and is like the "buried offer" in copy testing for print advertising. When consumers check or in some way mark the illustration with pencil or pen, they earn an extra bonus. But they learn what to do and what they receive only if they see the commercial. This added bit of information is usually very well received and enhances response.

Direct mail has a related device—a second letter in addition to the original direct mail letter. It doesn't work exactly like a transfer device, but it is an additional unit of information that increases response. This second, note-sized letter is intended to be read after the direct mail letter. It usually has a message that says something like: "Read this if you've decided not to take us up on our offer." Then it restates the offer and possibly extends an additional gift or bonus for promptness.

These notes come from left field. Just when you think you've read everything, along comes an extra bit of information. Sometimes this is just what it takes to tip the scale and get an order that might otherwise be lost. A note like this can boost response to a mailing by more than 10 percent.

The transfer device follows the same principle. Just when viewers think they've seen everything, they're hooked by a second lure. This similarity underscores the fact that direct marketers think consistently along certain lines and thus unconsciously tailor advertising media to fit their sales instincts. The direct mail writer and the response TV writer use time strategically. They are not solely concerned with *what* they have to say; they also care about *when* they can say it most effectively in order to produce action.

New Creative Quality

Another commercial that put direct response television on an equal footing with consumer advertising borrowed heavily from consumer advertising. It was a commercial for *Time* magazine by a Texas agency called the Richards Group. For the first time, the public saw a phone number on a commercial that was really different, exciting, and creative.

This innovative commercial featured many quick cuts and fast camera moves on still photographs, plus tricky little touches of animation. The fancy camera work was linked to witty, alliterative copy that read like breezy doggerel. The background music worked perfectly with the words and pictures. This tremendously appealing commercial was powerful and lighthearted at the same time. People talked about it; they watched it repeatedly for the fun of it. More important, they called an 800 number to order *Time* magazine.

The style of the Richards Group commercial was so successful and appealing that Time, Incorporated, used that style for four years to sell *Time* magazine and *Sports Illustrated*. This successful commercial encouraged other publishers to try their hands at creative direct response advertising. Response clients were finally demanding, and getting, the creative care to which consumer accounts had long been accustomed.

CBS Publications went on the air with highly successful commercials for *Field and Stream* and *Mechanix Illustrated*. These commercials departed creatively from the Richards Group style in that they incorporated live action with still photography. For *Field and Stream,* the live action showed a fisherman catching a fish. The action was broken into three sections—the fisherman casting, the fish striking, and the fisherman landing the fish—all in order to draw the viewer into the commercial so the idea of hauling the fish into the boat would synch up with the idea of hauling in a bargain by subscribing over the telephone. It worked.

Other magazines were advertised on television in the mid-1970s, including *Barrons, Bon Appétit, Consumer Reports, Ebony, Esquire, Essence, Fortune, Geo, Jet, Life, Money, Newsweek, Outdoor Life, Playboy, Rolling Stone,* and *U.S. News and World Report.* Many of these commercials were highly imaginative and quite different from anything that had gone before. But few could break free of a formula that consisted of a creative segment followed by a cut to a slide or an announcer in limbo for the sales pitch. Such an abrupt break in aesthetics might have done more harm than good. A better solution, and one that we are seeing more often these days, might have been to incorporate the announcer and his pitch tastefully within the main body of the commercial, thus preserving and strengthening the mood that was created to motivate response in the first place.

The Delayed Response

The last breakthrough in response television in the 1970s was Wunderman, Ricotta & Kline's transfer device, which was first used in 1977 in 60-second support commercials for the Columbia Record and Tape Club. Viewers were told to look for a special gold box in Columbia announcements that would appear in *TV Guide* and other publications. Viewers could write any Columbia record catalog number in the box and receive that record as a bonus. However, the information didn't appear in the print announcement; viewers only knew about the gold box if they saw the support commercial.

People responded enthusiastically. They liked being insiders and knowing something that others might not know. What started out as a gimmick to count heads and tally how many people had seen the commercial became a highly successful motivational technique. The transfer device upped response so much whenever it was used that it became a basic element in most support advertising. Commercial after commercial asked people to check, circle, or cross something out long after the surprise was gone.

The success of support commercials using transfer devices proved that viewers could make a direct response under rather complex circumstances. That is, something shown in a commercial had to be found somewhere else and acted upon in a specific way at some time in the future. In other words, support advertising was actually calling for a *delayed* direct response—a response in another medium at another time.

The implications are tremendous.

Everything that is packaged or labeled and sold on the shelf can be an advertisment that is triggered by support advertising. Support can turn a product into a direct response advertising medium. And that medium's message can set off a chain reaction. Buying something buys you the opportunity to sample something else and maybe get something delivered regularly to your home.

Most consumer goods commercials say little more than you're

going to like our product, so buy it. A delayed response commercial can say that easily, in addition to telling you to look for a direct response device on the label when you buy the product that will give you the chance to sample and purchase something else.

This is *mega-marketing*—a sell piled on a sell piled on a sell. And it all begins with a delayed response commercial, known as television support. If general advertising has fostered conspicuous consumption, then direct response advertising aims at *continuous* consumption. This has been a primary direct marketing goal because we've seen how one response can lead to another and yet another. Our declining economy calls for response advertising because as money buys increasingly less, success in business depends upon selling more goods continuously. The future belongs to direct marketing.

Direct Marketing Is the Future

To persons who are unfamiliar with direct marketing, response commercials can be a strange new animal. If you have never waited for the first orders to roll in after a commercial has run, you don't know the highs and lows that direct marketers experience. These highs and lows sharpen a response professional's selling instincts and ultimately serve to differentiate him or her from other ad people. We win or we lose. There is no ivory tower in which to hide. Who could be better equipped to handle America's advertising needs in the hard times ahead than the high-profile, one-hundred-percent accountable direct response pros?

Although it took more than 30 years, by 1980 direct response and support television emerged as the heir to the legacy of advertising in general. Only response can do something new and different nationally and multinationally. Dramatic progress in advertising is only possible through response because it is the only kind of advertising that has a real frontier ahead of it.

The interactive age has already dawned in the United States, Europe, and Japan. More distinguished companies are using direct response and support advertising on television, and their commercials look and sound better than direct response commercials ever have. That's going to make more customers out of skeptical consumers who believe that response is a questionable kind of advertising. By 1980, developments that looked like science fiction a few years before were figuring into direct response and support commercials. These developments will be discussed further on.

Response television has been moving like a wave that is gathering force. From a swell in the 1950s and '60s, it gained power and speed in the '70s, and is about to break in full force in the '80s for over 200 million television homes in the United States. Anyone who is on the crest of that wave is in for an incredible ride.

2
Response Television Today

Today's revolution in direct marketing is most evident in the way response commercials look. That is why we are looking at response television largely from the creative point of view. The TV audience reacts primarily to the creative side of direct marketing, a fact that professionals should also keep in mind.

It would be useful to start with a definition of response television that is broad enough to encompass everything the subject implies—so let's say that response television is simply television advertising concerned with direct marketing. It is presently used:

1. to sell products and services directly
2. to obtain sales leads
3. to support other forms of direct response advertising

Generally, a commercial for any of the listed uses is based on a *concept*—that is, a strong central idea that determines the look and sound of a commercial. For a long time, it was uncommon to base a response commercial on anything other than a demonstration. Most of them simply displayed the product and/or demonstrated its benefits or uses and that was it. But the growing influence of general advertising has led to many more commercials that utilize concepts other than the product's features or benefits.

Advertising professionals come up with concepts by considering the benefits a product seems to offer, along with the emotional need it seems to satisfy, such as the desire to be young, beautiful, happy, loved, secure, intelligent, respected, independent, or strong. The more simple the concept is, the greater its impact will be. For instance, the slogan, "Have a Coke and a smile," implies that Coca-Cola tastes good (the benefit) and that drinking Coke will make you happy (the satisfied emotional need). The only difference between a concept such as this one gleaned from general advertising and a concept used in response advertising is that a good response concept will also tell the viewer to do something now, in addition to stating a benefit and promising to satisfy an emotional need.

Every response commercial has one overriding purpose—it must produce action. If it is a *direct* response commercial, it must stimulate people to move from a sitting position to a standing position. This is more important than making a product look good, and it is more important than presenting stirring words and beautiful pictures, although these may be ways of moving people to action. The objective of a direct response commercial is to make the TV viewer stop what he or she is doing, stand up, and order the product. *He* may have to put down his can of beer and leave his chair. *She* may have to stop reading. *They* may have to stop playing cards. So response commercials are special. They not only have to offer benefits and appeal to needs; they must make people move.

People usually move because they want to be sold something in the first place. They don't necessarily want particular products, but they do want the dreams that accompany those products. They have come to believe that products will instantly satisfy their emotional needs. The economic trials of the 1980s may challenge this notion, but for the moment, Americans still believe that money buys happiness and that happiness is equated with consumer goods.

But the audience still calls the shots when it comes to selling products on television. The audience determines what is sold and how it is sold because products are sold only when the advertiser strikes a responsive chord. Advertising is not an elite craft; it is a social reflection of the wishes of ordinary people—their dreams, needs, fears, and self-images. A commercial merely objectifies what was in the consumer's mind in the first place. All you are doing when you sell something is giving someone back a part of himself. And the surest way to achieve that in a commercial is to start with a solid concept.

It is probably true that the product, the offer, and the creative execution stand in that order of importance in making sales. But the concept is the creative tissue that holds these elements together, and a response commercial without a solid concept is a primitive and stunted effort.

Direct Response Commercials

When response television is used to sell products and services directly, the commercials fall into two categories:

1. the one-shot—a commercial that sells one product once through television
2. continuity—a commercial promoting the sale of a series of installments

The basic direct response sales unit for television is two minutes, although many direct response commercials can say what they have to say in 60 seconds. A two-minute unit is usually required to sell continuity, and some one-shot offers are so complicated that they also require two minutes. Two minutes of TV time is expensive, however, sometimes too expensive to make a TV commercial cost-efficient. The less you pay for TV time, the fewer orders you need to make a profit. The lower your cost is per thousand viewers, the better your chances are for success. Also, sometimes two-minute spots are simply unavailable. Stations won't sell them if their time is in high demand and short supply, as it can be around national elections and preceding Christmas. Ninety-second commercials have been used occasionally, but their success rate has been poor and they usually cost as much as a two-minute spot.

One-Shot Commercials

Many of today's direct response one-shots are "sixties" and are structured as direct response commercials have been for the past 30 years. A typical direct response commercial starts by grabbing the viewer's attention. If there's a free gift, the commercial may follow up the opening with the gift or save mention of it until just before the ordering information at the end. After the attention-getting opening, the commercial states the premise in one or two sentences. The bulk of the commercial demonstrates the product or discusses its attributes. The last, or "legal," part of the commercial gives the cost of the product, the shipping and handling charges (if any), the suggested retail value, the savings (if there is a discount), and the delivery time.

Ordering information is usually combined with or precedes the single most important part of any direct response commercial —the telephone number and, if there is one, the ordering address. This nuts-and-bolts copy can be incorporated in the body of the commercial, but it is usually saved for the end—for the moment of truth when the telephone number appears. If viewers have been sufficiently stimulated, they will pay attention to this part of the commercial, get the facts, and then order.

A Common Formula. Because of the inbred nature of direct response advertising, the kind of selling it has to do, and the logic this kind of selling generates, something like a formula for direct response commercials has evolved. It can be outlined in a diagram.

Classic 60-Second Direct Response Commercial

A	B	C	D
5	10–15	30	15

The elements of the direct response commercial are:

1. Attention-getting opening (about 5 seconds)
2. Premise and/or mention of premium (up to 15 seconds)
3. Product display, possibly with premium (30 seconds)
4. Ordering information and telephone number (15 seconds)

Naturally there is room for considerable variation within this formula as can be seen in the examples in Figures 2–1 through 2–6 on pages 41–52.

These commercials have many points in common that typify direct response advertising—they offer a bargain, guarantee satisfaction, and make the product easy to order. In other words, they make shopping at home easy, convenient, safe, and economical. Like the creative portion of the commercial, all these marketing points are intended to produce action, that is, to get a direct response. Creativity stimulates the customer and the marketing elements reassure him. The mixture produces action.

The principal element in all direct response commercials is the means of ordering, which is a telephone number and/or a write-in address. This is the aesthetically unappealing part of most of today's direct response commercials. It is also the most important part, the convenience-shopping part, the part that echoes the old direct mail argument about the desirability of shopping "in the comfort of one's own home."

Everything else in a response commercial is a prologue to the telephone number, which is comparable to the coupon in direct response print advertising and the order card in direct mail. That telephone number has one job to do. It makes it easy to order the advertised product. This is essential because direct marketers know that people will not go out of their way to order. They must be told precisely how to order and given the simplest means to do so. (Incidentally, mnemonic telephone numbers that spell out the name of a product or service, such as 800-VITAMIN, usually don't perform as well as ordinary, uncomplicated telephone numbers like 800-555-1000.)

No strict rule governs the use of a write-in address. Using an address depends on the product, the market, and the offer. For instance, a certain percentage of some markets will usually order only by mail. (Elderly customers, for example, tend to write in.) What's more, if it is advisable to ask for cash, viewers can send payment with a write-in order. Although it may be unusual nowadays to ask for a check or money order up front, there are times when this may be desirable, particularly when you are using television to generate orders stemming from radical-impulse buyers or from an unreliable market. One new ploy to get a customer's cash commitment is to ask for postage and handling payment up front.

According to Errol Davis, President of Communication Response Service, Inc., in an article on telephone marketing in the 1979 *Direct Mail/Marketing Manual,* "a successful TV offer will produce 60 to 80 percent of its orders via toll-free phone, the balance coming prepaid by mail." So the telephone is the way to get the most orders, but you get significant amounts of cash up front when you offer a write-in option.

The Toll-Free Number. Toll-free numbers (800 numbers) have been around for more than a decade. The service is known as Wide Area Telephone Service (WATS), a bulk phone service purchased in advance that covers specific geographic areas. WATS is an obvious boon to direct marketing, but it can pose problems. For one thing, the quality of customers who call toll-free is usually lower than the quality of those obtained through print or mail. Depending on the product or the offer, there are always a certain number of customers who won't pay their bills or who will refuse to pay the COD charges on products they have ordered. But bad debt risks are always a problem where impulse buying is concerned. If you anticipate a payment problem, don't ship the goods. Send the customer a note of acknowledgment with a bill before shipping the product. If you have a premium, specify in your commercial that it will be sent with *paid* orders. Invite viewers to use their credit cards. These extra qualifiers will eliminate some of your orders, but you'll get a higher quality customer.

There are problems in handling toll-free calls themselves, especially when your commercial is a winner. Davis explains that most toll-free phone centers that handle in-coming calls operate seven days a week and are staffed to handle anticipated phone volume. Of course, a "hot" product marketed on TV can cause an unexpected number of calls into a toll-free center resulting in some of the callers having to re-dial one or two more times to order. This is a sometimes necessary occurrence, particularly where TV and other voice media are utilized and the "high powered" commercials urge the viewer to "call now for this limited offer—operators are waiting to take your call!" This may be true, unless there are more callers than either lines or operators.

A national TV offer, especially during prime time, is another promotion that brings fear and anger to the heart of "Ma Bell." A major automobile manufacturer succeeded in knocking out most long distance communications to one section of the United States for several hours when a free brochure was advertised during a prime time sports event, due to the heavy call volume into the WATS center. While thousands of brochures were ordered, more than 10,000 callers failed to reach the center due to the heavy number of callers trying to reach the "waiting operators" who were, in fact, unable to handle the unexpected call volume.

It's easy to see why careful planning is essential when you're providing a toll-free number. The administration behind the scenes has to be experienced and professional. And when the number is on the screen, it has to be there long enough to register with the viewers. Experience shows that fifteen seconds is the least amount of time the number must appear on the screen in a one-minute commercial. For a two-minute commercial it's twenty seconds. There is a measurable drop-off in response proportionate to every second less than the basic fifteen and twenty. It's also advisable for the announcer to say the phone number at least three times during the commercial. Don't be afraid to keep repeating the number—it is that important. It's also the part of the commercial that brands response television as a crass medium, but it needn't be that way. Toll-free numbers are being used more imaginatively than ever these days. Some are animated and integrated very creatively within the body of the commercial, and others appear and disappear teasingly within commercials.

Local telephone numbers are also used to take orders in direct response commercials. Sometimes it's cheaper to use a local service than an 800 number, particularly when a market is localized and is not likely to be nationwide. Furthermore, tests have shown that more people ordered through a local number than a toll-free number when two numbers for ordering the same product were tested in comparable markets. This is not enough reason to generalize in favor of using local numbers, however.

Make It a Bargain. In addition to telephone numbers that make it easy to order, price is another key factor in marketing direct through television. Mail-order shoppers like bargains and discounts. They like to save money. So the prices for direct response TV offers are often discount prices or bargain prices below retail. Also, they are often expressed as a dollar amount plus *ninety-five cents,* because people still feel better about paying five cents less than a price that seems to be a dollar more.

For some time now the rule of thumb for one-shots has been that $14.95 is the upper limit the mass audience is willing to spend on a TV product. What the response-buying public doesn't accept one year, however, it may accept the next. That top limit of $14.95 is now in the process of becoming $19.95. Small wonder, then, that prices ought to be tested on television as assiduously as they are in mail and print.

Attitudes change. At one time people were reluctant to call 800 numbers. Even the words "toll-free call" didn't make it clear that the call didn't cost the customer a cent. Enough commercials had to say "the call is free" before the idea sank in. Now most (although not all) home shoppers make toll-free calls without hesitation.

Customers used to have a similar reluctance to making credit card purchases. When commercials began to invite viewers to use their credit cards to make direct response TV purchases, people were afraid to give their card numbers over the telephone. That has changed. In fact, making certain TV products, such as calculators and watches, available *only* through the use of a credit card has turned out to be one way of moving high-ticket items successfully. Direct response commercials for expensive products under $100 were successful when they were pitched to "credit card holders only." This indicates that credit card holders are more likely to buy expensive products since, as a class of customers, they have higher incomes and more discretionary capital than non-credit card holders. They are safer customers because they have been credit-checked in advance. And many of them still don't think of their cards as real money, so they tend to spend freely.

If there's one thing that direct response customers like better than bargains and discounts, it's a free gift. The gift that is free (when you buy something else) has been so effective that it has dominated the creative direction of numerous major direct marketing operations for years. Even the introductory offers of the mail-order record clubs are variations of the free-gift approach, like the one that invites you to take 13 records or tapes for one penny for becoming a member. The appeal of a premium should be considered when planning inexpensive one-shots for television because people, particularly direct response shoppers, have never stopped wanting something for nothing. But remember that direct marketing operations of high caliber, such as the Franklin Mint, have been able to avoid the use of premiums. By not using premiums and thereby avoiding the clutter a premium brings to a promotion, their advertising has a clean look that is desirable on television where the creative goal is simplicity.

Satisfaction Guaranteed. People want bargains and gifts, but they are still suspicious about getting something for nothing. Direct marketers have to go out of their way to assure customers that it is safe to order. Satisfaction *must* be guaranteed. The customers have to know that they can try before they buy and that their money will be refunded or they need not pay at all if they are not delighted. This guarantee is a legal requirement; but even if it weren't, it would be good business to offer a money-back guarantee to counteract customers' natural skepticism. Besides, money-back guarantees are usually a safe bet. They make people secure enough to order, but even dissatisfied customers don't always take the time to return a product in order to get their money back.

Often in direct response print advertising, and almost always in direct mail, a guarantee of satisfaction is set in type surrounded by a fancy, official-looking certificate border. It assures the customer that he can examine the merchandise on a free-trial basis and return it without paying anything if he is not completely satisfied. On television this kind of information is usually relayed in a simple sentence like: "Satisfaction guaranteed or your money back" or simply "Satisfaction guaranteed!"

Less assurance is needed when the product has an established image, such as a nationally distributed magazine that is using television to obtain new subscribers. But direct response products tend to be exclusive items. As the commercials say, they are not available in stores. This exclusivity is a big selling point because the product can be obtained only through responding to the commercial. But since the product isn't out there on the shelf competing with other products and available for comparison and personal examination, words of reassurance are called for.

Continuity Programs

Everything just mentioned about selling one-shots on television applies doubly to continuity programs, except that continuity programs are not hit-or-miss propositions. Satisfaction has to be guaranteed in more than words. The first installment received has to be satisfying enough to encourage the customer to stay in the program. One-shot products are filmed to look their best on television; but when the customer receives them, they often fall short of the way they look on the screen. Lighting and camera angles are cosmetics that make what's small seem large, what's tacky seem elegant. But a continuity commercial, as well as the initial installment it promotes, should spell quality that can be delivered.

In continuity programs, merchandise comes to the customer in regular shipments. Typical programs are series of books, records, art prints, collectors' items, medallic art, and instructional or informative cards. The first offering in any series is normally available for free examination. It should be of the same quality as other offerings in the series, but it can usually be purchased at an introductory price that is much lower than the price of future installments. Sometimes it is an outright gift. Sometimes one or more premiums also go with the first installment.

The idea is to hook the customer with a bargain, hoping that by opening the door in this way, much more of the product can be sold later on, or at the "back end" as the money-making part of a continuity program is called. Making money in continuity depends not only on how many customers will respond to the advertising initially, but also on how many of these customers will remain in the program and for how long.

The Basic Structure. Continuity programs can be open or closed—they can contain a specific number of installments or the installments can continue indefinitely, as long as the demand exists. Most continuity programs that obtain members through TV commercials do not require a minimum purchase. Customers can withdraw from the program at any time after informing the company of their decision in writing.

A commercial selling a continuity program should explain the program and get a direct response from viewers requesting a free examination of the initial installment. The time formula for a typical continuity commercial is much like the formula for a direct response one-shot commercial, but more details must be included.

Classic 120-Second Continuity Commercial

A	B	C	D	E	F
5–10	15	40	20	10	20

The elements of the continuity commercial are:

1. Opening and premise (5 to 10 seconds)
2. Introduction of series (15 seconds)
3. Dramatization of series (40 seconds)
4. First installment display (20 seconds)
5. Premiums, if any (position variable—10 seconds)
6. Terms of offer, ordering instructions, telephone number (20 seconds)

Any or all of the elements in any commercial can be manipulated. For instance, continuity commercials often open with free gifts. We are describing one-shot and continuity commercials in terms of a formula to show the kind of commercial that is seen most often today. The formulas that have evolved are not engraved in stone. Many current exceptions to these formulas prove that the creative future is unlimited.

The Sell That Keeps on Selling. Direct response continuity commercials can be thought of as the sell that keeps on selling. All the additional purchases these programs encourage begin with one commercial asking people to try one installment. There are no subsequent commercials to improve the back end performance. Nevertheless, if the commercial is done well enough in the first place, it can have that effect. The continuity commercial does a lot of work, so it shouldn't be surprising that it's quite a job to make one of these specialized commercials work well. But it's worth it.

A continuity commercial has a lot of explaining to do: it has to encourage the trial of a first installment; it might have to tout premiums; and it has to create a favorable impression of an entire program. The result is that much of the commercial is taken up by dull, nonmotivating legal-type copy. And with so much to say, it's not surprising that most continuity commercials are two minutes long. Sixty-second versions of two-minute continuity commercials have been tested with little success. Although more testing needs to be done, two minutes is still the basic unit of TV time for continuity.

When continuity commercials were new, products like the

Betty Crocker Recipe Card File and Safari Cards from the Margrace Corporation sold well. But resistance is increasing. People have finally realized that they can end up spending a lot of money if they get involved in a continuity program. The average continuity card program, for instance, takes editorial material that might cost the consumer $20 if purchased in book form, puts it on cards, divides the cards into installments, provides a box to put the installments in, and charges a few dollars for each installment . . . month after month after month. Or there may be a "load-up," in which the customer receives installments in bulk but continues to be billed a regular monthly installment fee. Either way, if the customer stays in the program long enough, the costs mount astronomically. He or she can end up paying more than $100 for the same material that would be reasonably inexpensive as a book. This is one of those direct marketing "catches" again, and customers are wising up to it. All the free gifts used as bait aren't going to change that awareness.

A good product doesn't need a free gift to sell it. Time-Life, Inc., has a reputation and products that spell quality to the mass audience. The books in a Time-Life series are so interesting and so handsomely produced that home delivery in regular installments is seen as a real benefit. Consequently, there have been occasions when Time-Life has been able to sell its libraries with continuity commercials that offer no free gifts—only a free examination of the first volume. This is what continuity sales *should* be like, and it's no surprise that Time-Life commercials reflect the quality of the products they sell. Inevitably, the quality of the commercial equals the quality of the product, which in turn equals the quality of the customer.

Profitable continuity programs are difficult to arrive at; but still the idea of the sell that goes on selling is so promising that continuity is a first-class priority for direct marketers. Direct marketing, which allows you to shop at home and have products delivered to your home, has been accurately described as the kind of marketing that turns products into services; and this is precisely the case with continuity. The commercial explains everything you need to know about the program. Your initial response to the commercial by telephone is followed by regular home delivery of the product in installments. This saves you the time and the trouble of ever having to shop for that product again. Imagine what that could mean if the product was beer or toilet paper—but let's save that for the next chapter.

Magazine subscriptions are not discussed here because subscriptions sold through television aren't continuity sales. A TV-sold magazine subscription is a great example of a product becoming a service. But the subscriber doesn't get a bill for each new issue, he can't buy some issues and not others, and he can't opt for a load-up, all of which he could do in a real continuity program. (See Figures 2–7 and 2–8 on pages 52–56).

Gathering Leads

Direct response commercials are used to get sales leads when a product or service is quite expensive or when something is too complicated to explain and sell in two minutes. The idea behind these commercials is to get the viewer to call for more information.

This approach is frequently taken by trade, technical, and correspondence schools. Medical and legal clinics also use it. So do companies that market therapeutic devices for use in the home. The military has produced many lead-generating commercials that end with the phone numbers of recruiting offices. Tourist boards use lead-gathering commercials to get their brochures into circulation, as do public service agencies, although they are not necessarily looking for a commitment or a conversion.

A typical commercial for sales leads starts with a consumer problem or benefit and closes with a telephone number and possibly an address.

Classic 30-Second Lead-Gathering Commercial

A	B	C
5–10	10–20	10–15

The elements of the lead-gathering commercial are:

1. Statement of benefit or a problem (5 to 10 seconds)
2. Dramatization (10 to 20 seconds)
3. Telephone number and/or address (10 to 15 seconds)

The viewer who responds to a lead-gathering commercial either will get a brochure or his call will be returned by a salesperson. Usually the customer will receive a brochure first, and then a salesperson makes a follow-up call several days later.

The issues here are leads and conversions: How many people

will the commercial get to call in? How many of those people can be converted into customers? Conversions depend upon the quality of the leads obtained and the efficacy of the follow-up. So any commercial created to obtain leads has to know exactly to whom it is speaking.

Moreover, a residual effect can be important here, and the commercial should be written with the conversion process in mind. A good commercial can fix an image in the viewer's mind, which a salesperson cannot do and a brochure is not likely to do. Images from a commercial have an extended lifespan, living in the viewer's mind and working for a long time after the commercial has been seen. Consequently, particularly vivid lead-gathering commercials can help in the conversion process—especially if a key phrase, image, or concept from the commercial is used in the follow-up. For instance, the headline of a brochure might be a slogan from television, or a salesperson might refer to a commercial's main points when talking to a sales prospect—after all, the lead-gathering commercial is virtually the foot in the door. If the commercial happens to be running the day of the week the salesperson calls, the reinforcement is certainly an advantage.

Direct marketing is, by nature, a step by step proposition. For instance, a commercial leads to a brochure, which leads to a sales call and, finally, to a sales agreement. There should be conceptual and thematic unity every step of the way. Too often there isn't. And that is regrettable since it has been shown repeatedly that consumers who are being sold a product tend to concentrate on only one or two simple ideas. If those simple ideas are working strongly enough in the commercial to obtain the lead in the first place, it stands to reason that they should be put to work all the way down the line.

When we talk about obtaining leads, of course we're talking about *qualified* leads, good prospects rather than a lot of meaningless names that a strong but off-target commercial can generate. Remember that the quality of respondents obtained through television is usually inferior to those generated through direct mail and print. But dollars spent on TV advertising buy more people than the same money would buy in mail. And TV works faster than mail. It has a unique immediacy and excitement that produces results in the form of leads and orders in greater bulk than any other advertising medium. Response commercials simply need fine tuning when they are created to get the right response from the right people. (See Figures 2–9 and 2–10 on pages 57–60).

Support Advertising

Now we come to TV support advertising. Support doesn't try to sell viewers anything directly. Rather, it tells them to look for some other piece of advertising that's coming their way. The advertising that does try to sell you something is called the *primary medium*. Support is accomplished through the *secondary medium*. Technically, any medium can support another and how they are combined is determined by cost efficiency. For instance, television commercials have supported postcards that have supported direct mail packages. Some combinations of media have barely been explored; others have never been attempted. In this chapter we are concerned only with today's TV support: commercials used to promote print ads, newspapers inserts, and direct mail.

When to Use Support

The job of support is to sell the advertising piece that does the selling. Support creates excitement and anticipation about what's coming. It rolls out a red carpet. And it works! *Support advertising can increase response to a direct mail or a direct response print effort by anywhere from 10 to 70 percent.* Of course, not every advertiser can use support. It is part of a costly two-pronged sales approach that calls for considerable testing and analysis before and after a support commercial gets on the air. The companies that have been able to afford support campaigns have been mass mailers such as Xerox, *Reader's Digest,* Unity Buying Service, and the magazine subscription agency Publishers Clearing House —all of whom drop millions of pieces of advertising in the mail at a shot. Or they have been companies like Time-Life Books and the RCA and Columbia record clubs with big budgets to spend on magazine inserts and newspaper preprints.

As a result of their very successful support campaigns for Publishers Clearing House, McCann-Erickson March, Inc. stresses two factors that will determine whether an advertiser can use TV support.

1. The product or service sold in the primary medium must have mass appeal.
2. The primary medium has to reach no less than 25 percent of its market. If it doesn't, television support would be too costly and should be ruled out.

If the above criteria are met, an advertiser would do well to include a TV support campaign in his marketing plan and test it, just as he would test his primary advertising. The aim of the support campaign is to make the primary direct response advertising as efficient as possible. Some of the criteria determining whether support advertising can maximize that efficiency have been described in the current *Direct Mail/Marketing Manual* by Tom Knowlton, Executive Vice President of Wunderman, Ricotta & Kline. They are:

1. Cost of the primary medium
2. Precision of delivery of the primary medium
3. Distribution of the primary medium providing high penetration areas
4. Cost of the support medium
5. Expected improvement in pull

After the cost of a support campaign is determined, most of the planning goes into assuring that the support commercial will run often enough to register before the viewer receives the primary medium. Television is a great medium for support because it can reach more people in less time than any other medium. On an average, a television set is turned on for more than seven hours a day in 98 percent of American households. Support tries to reach a predetermined number of those households when and as often as it has been deemed necessary to call favorable attention to a primary medium.

When, Where, and How Often

The two terms that are used most often in media planning for support campaigns are *reach* and *frequency*. Reach is the percentage of unduplicated households that will see a commercial during its run. Frequency is the number of times those households will see the commercial. The marketing objective determines the amount and proportion of reach and frequency for each support campaign; and in this strategic use of media, direct marketing relies heavily on the experience of general advertising.

Anyone who has been in on the planning that determines reach and frequency in a support campaign has to admire the people who decide when, where, and how many times a commercial should be aired in order to do its job. The when, where, and how many times are as important in their way to the commercial's success as the creative portion is. Similarly, a parallel can be drawn between the success of a direct mail package based on its list selection and the success of a support campaign based on its media plan. Support strategy has everything to do with buying sufficient time in the right markets at an efficient cost. This, like determining how many WATS lines to reserve for a response commercial, is knowledge gained through experience.

In buying time for TV support, we have to trust the experience of seasoned media buyers, who buy time in units called *gross rating points,* which are measures of reach and frequency. One rating point equals one percent of the households in a market, whether it is a national market or a regional market. The number of gross rating points for any support campaign depends on the product being sold and its marketing plan; therefore, the number varies from campaign to campaign. There are, however, firm guidelines governing when a support commercial should run.

With support for direct mail, it is important to remember that it's impossible to pinpoint the exact day a mailing will be delivered. So a commercial supporting a mailing, which we guess will be delivered on Monday, will run on Friday, Saturday, Sunday, and Monday. But the commercial will also continue through the following Thursday, just in case the mail is delayed.

Knowing when to air commercials that support a Sunday newspaper insert is much easier. Since we know the insert will be published on Sunday, experience indicates that the best schedule for TV support is to start on Friday evening, go right through Saturday and Saturday evening, and run a bit during the daytime on Sunday for added insurance. Saturday is clearly the most important day and night to run; the extra time is used simply to reach as many people as possible. The people creating the support commercial should keep this timing in mind because it gives a fuller picture of the circumstances under which their message will be exposed, which should have a decided effect on the look and sound of the commercial.

Support commercials are usually 30 or 60 seconds long. Thirty- and sixty-second versions of the same commercial are frequently produced and tested. These commercials have only three points to make: (1) they tell you *what* to look for, (2) *when* to expect it, and (3) *where* to expect it.

The support commercials currently seen on television ask viewers to watch the mail for a special offer or to look for one in the Sunday paper. They don't try to convince them to buy the paper. They assume that viewers will get it on Sunday and, when they find the insert, they will remember the support commercial.

Creating Recognition

The "star" of any support commercial is the tangible advertisement being supported—the insert, ad, preprint, or direct mail package that does the actual selling. There shouldn't be any doubt about this point. The support commercial will probably refer to the offer in the ad it is supporting, but this reference is secondary. The important point is that viewers recognize and anticipate the actual piece of paper that is coming their way. Any support commercial is going to be less efficient if sufficient attention is not devoted to what the primary medium looks like and where and when it is going to turn up. The principle is similar to new-product advertising. New products aren't familiar, so launch commercials have to show off the packaging. Likewise, what's coming through the mail or in the Sunday paper is also unfamiliar, so the support commercial has to make it vivid and memorable. The primary advertising material has to be on camera long enough for viewers to recognize it when they find it at home. It also has to be presented interestingly enough to make people care about getting it.

A typical modern support commercial can be diagrammed simply.

Classic 60-Second Support Commercial

A	B
10–30	30–50

The elements of the support commercial are:

1. Dramatization of proposition (10 to 30 seconds)
2. Facts about the primary medium (30 to 50 seconds)

The stimulating part of a good support commercial can come from the theme or the offer contained in what's being supported; but the excitement should focus on the physical advertisement the commercial is supporting. Consequently, the primary material will become magical and desirable because it contains all of the drama, excitement, and benefits of what it is selling. Figure 2–11 on pages 61–62 is an effective example from Time-Life Books illustrating this point.

This Time-Life commercial did justice to the preprints it

supported. It enhanced the preprint with sound and motion, which made the preprint seem more "important" to people who had seen the commercials. A good commercial adds dignity and dimension to the direct mail and coupon ads that many people hold in low esteem. A good commercial about direct mail or a preprint suddenly lifts the curse because television is regarded as a quality advertising medium. (See Figure 2–12 on pages 62–63).

Support does more for the primary medium as well. It creates a multiple impression of what is being sold, thus providing reinforcement for a stronger sell. "Ah," says the consumer, when he finds the newspaper insert he had been prepared to find, "here's that ad I saw on television." At this stage of the game, the support commercial works like an echo. While the consumer is reading the ad, he might be replaying some of the support commercial in his mind's eye. At this point, everything that was good and emphatic about the commercial will be working double-time to produce a response.

If the support commercial accomplishes its first objective, the consumer will recognize the primary medium and think it is special. If the commercial is really good, it will successfully combine image-making with action-producing techniques to encourage a delayed direct response.

Action Devices

Direct marketers know that action devices, such as affixable YES/NO tokens in direct mail packages, encourage people to act. When such devices can be included in the announcement being supported, they can be used to make the support commercial highly motivating, as in the following example from Unity Buying Service.

Unity mails millions of self-mailers nationwide at a single drop. The self-mailers feature a die-cut window in front with a perforated, detachable membership card showing through. Because a valid Unity membership card could mean discounts of up to 50 percent and more on thousands of nationally advertised products, the most important part of Unity's support commercial is that highly visible membership card. The goal was to motivate the viewer to want that card. It was reasonable to assume that once the viewer detached the card himself, Unity as good as had another customer. So the support commercial encourages the viewer to detach the card by magnifying that action on television.

The commercial opens with the membership card filling the screen. A hand detaches the card while a sound effect amplifies the sound of the card ripping free. The camera pulls back to show the whole self-mailer. Then we see an announcer holding the self-mailer and the card. He tells us that the Unity card can get us the things we want, and then he gestures with the card and products appear magically. The rest of the commercial explains Unity's offer and tells the viewer to watch for the mailing—all in 30 seconds. (See Figure 2–13 on page 64).

The theory behind the commercial is that people will want to do the things they see being done on television. The Unity commercial fulfills the first responsibility of support in that it focuses on the primary medium. But it went a step further. It used film to lend sound and motion to the primary medium, which the self-mailer could not do for itself. So this commercial may have actually helped to *produce* the delayed direct response.

Support commercials don't have to be highly directive to be effective; they needn't shout *do this*. They can try to produce action as subtly as the Unity commercial did. The Unity commercial didn't tell anyone to do anything with that membership card—it simply featured a particular act and let viewers come to their own conclusions. And what could be better than when a viewer's own conclusions, arrived at "independently," are the marketer's conclusions as well? A person who thinks that he is making up his own mind will be a better customer than someone who is pushed into acting. Commercials that stimulate independent thinking are also likely to produce customers who will be more favorably disposed to a product and purchase more of it than commercials that do not encourage customers to come to their own conclusions—an important consideration when you think about the significance of the back end in many direct marketing programs.

Direct response, lead-gathering, and support commercials look better than ever because direct marketing savvy and efficiency have finally linked with general advertising slickness. This was inevitable and, for a time, response commercials are going to look more like consumer spots. They will be more interesting, exciting, and fun to watch because talented people with general agency backgrounds will help to create them and will encourage more money to be spent on their production. This is a necessary and welcome phase of response advertising—but it is only a phase.

The next chapter looks at future commercials and how what's happening now—the mingling of general advertising and response advertising—will help determine the future. But there is no last word. Today the best response commercials are hybrids—they have the characteristics of their parent forms of advertising, but they are distinctive in and of themselves. Response commercials of the future could be entirely different after we pass through this period of hybridization. What happens will have as much or more to do with the technology that creates and conveys response advertising as it will with the creative background. Understanding, then, that the future is something that exists for us now only in outline, we can move ahead to the next chapter where something that may resemble the future is waiting.

FIGURE 2-1. Demonstration is the big gun in response television's creative arsenal. Dial Marketing's two-minute commercial for the Ginsu knife is nonstop demonstration and display beginning with a strong concept that even accommodates a joke. Everything a good direct response commercial can have is here. © Ginsu Products, Inc.

In Japan, the hand can be used like a knife . . .

but this method doesn't work

with a tomato,

that's why we use the Ginsu. It's a knife

that no kitchen should be without.

The Ginsu can cut a slice of bread so thin,

you can almost see through it.

It cuts meat better than an electric knife,

and goes through frozen food as though it were melted butter. The Ginsu is so sharp,

it can cut through a tin can . . .

It can chop wood and still remain razor sharp.

How much would you pay for a knife like this? Before you answer . . . listen.

It even comes with a matching fork to make carving a pleasure. Wait! There's much, much more.

We also want you to have this six-in-one kitchen tool.

It peels and slivers carrots,

peels potatoes, and slices paper-thin potato chips.

This amazing little knife even grates cheese,

and makes beautiful decorative vegetables.

How much would you pay for all these items?

Well, we'll even give you this set of six precision steak knives . . .

And to make the offer completely irresistible, you'll get this unique spiral slicer . . .

down and down, around and around,

and you'll have a beautiful garnish for your dinner table.

Now, how much would you pay?

You get the Ginsu Knife,

the matching carving fork, the versatile six-in-one kitchen tool,

a set of six steak knives

and the spiral slicer . . .

You get them all guaranteed in writing for 50 years, for only $9.95.

It's the most incredible knife offer ever.

To order, call toll free 1-800-228-2035 . . . save the COD charges, send $9.95 to: Knife Set, Box 833, Radio City Station, New York, N.Y. 10019. You get the Ginsu Knife, matching carving fork, six-in-one kitchen tool, six steak knives and spiral slicer, plus a 50-year guarantee. So send $9.95 to: Knife Set, Box 833, Radio City Station, New York. Be sure to order yours today.

FIGURE 2-2.   TV's longest-running commercial is this one by Vista Marketing. It has outlived the actor, John Williams, and has gone through several changes in price to keep pace with inflation. © Vista Marketing

I'm sure you recognize this lovely melody, "Stranger In Paradise," but did you know that

the original theme is from the Polovetsian Dance No. 2 by Borodin? So many of the melodies of well-known popular songs

were actually written by the great masters—like these familiar themes—

(SOUND OF "Our Love")

(SOUND OF "Full Moon and Empty Arms")

(SOUND OF "Tonight We Love")

And now, all of the best-loved melodies from the classics

have been gathered by Vista Marketing into a big four-record collection.

Yes, here are a hundred and twenty of the greatest works from Strauss, Beethoven, Schubert, and many more

performed by Europe's finest musicians.

It's a priceless introduction to the classics that will enrich every home,

and it's all yours for only $9.98.

But there's a great deal more.

You also get this special collection of Piano Masterpieces—

thirty of the most beautiful melodies ever composed for the keyboard.

So, altogether you get a hundred and fifty of the world's greatest music masterpieces—all for only $9.98.

This collection is also available on 8-track cartridges for only $12.98.

Yes, here's a unique opportunity to own a complete library of the world's most beautiful music.

Here's how to order yours.

ANNOUNCER 2: To order, 'phone 265-3366; that's 265-3366, or save COD charges by sending $9.98 for records, $12.98 for

FIGURE 2-3. Note the toll-free number up front in this 60-second spot by Dom Cerulli for the Bell System's "Big Hello" gift certificates. Many versions for associated Bell System companies were created by changing the phone numbers and logos in the frames where they appear. It is, in effect, a national spot that ran regionally with local numbers. Client: AT & T. Agency: AyerDirect, division of N W Ayer ABH International. © AT & T

VO: The Bell System has a . . . new way to say hello—

"BIG HELLO" Telephone Gift Certificates.

People everywhere are calling this number to order the gift that just can't miss.

"BIG HELLO" Gift Certificates . . . the gift you can give anyone to use anytime.
DGHTR: Hello . . .

MOTHER: Hi, Kathy. I just got your "BIG HELLO."
DGHTR: It's a telephone Gift Certificate, Mom. Use it to call Gene in Europe . . .

or add special features to your phone service. Or . . .
MOTHER: Or I can treat myself to that fancy phone I told you about.

DGHTR: What a terrific idea!
VO: "BIG HELLO" Gift Certificates come

in convenient amounts, along with this holiday envelope for you to personalize. Simply include the gift certificate with the phone bill and the amount will be deducted automatically.

They're as easy to give as money, but much more personal. SFX: (BEEPS)
MOTHER: Hi Eugene, it's Mom!

Order extras for last minute gifts.

Call this number now. Avoid the holiday crunch. There are no postage or handling charges. Bell telephone customers . . . ask about charging them to your phone bill. Call now.

FIGURE 2-4.   Some of the best-looking and most imaginative direct response commercials are created for the telephone company's Dial-It services. This thirty-second short story by writer Stan Baum blends direct marketing with general advertising. Client: New York Telephone. Agency: Wunderman, Ricotta & Kline. © New York Telephone

(EERIE HIGH VIOLIN MUSIC)

(MAN GROANING)

(SFX)

(MUSIC, SFX)

ANNCR: (VO) When you're turning into a bit of a grouch . . .

(ROAR OF WOLFMAN)
. . . that's the time

for Dial-A-Joke.

(MUSIC UNDER)
(SFX DIALING)

(SFX: GROWLING)
Dial 976-3838.

(SFX, LAUGHING) It could
change your outlook
completely.

Dial-A-Joke, 976-3838. You'll
feel like your old self again.

(MUSIC OUT)

FIGURE 2-5.   Here the free gift is right up front and provides the opening in this two-minute direct response commercial for *Outdoor Life*. Note the telephone number used early on to signal that the customer can make a toll-free call. Client: Times Mirror Magazines. Agency: Grey Direct. © Times Mirror Magazines

(MUSIC-UNDER)
MAN: You can see it in their
eyes. They are some of the
most dangerous animals in
the world.

The lion—if it's hungry, it will
eat you.

The leopard—it's a deadly
killer because it's small and
almost totally silent.

The grizzly—it stands nine feet tall. Now you can come face to face with them in this special gift from Outdoor Life.

Incredible stories on the animals that strike the deepest terror in man.

It's the <u>Most Dangerous Game</u>—from the editors of Outdoor Life—

a special <u>free</u> gift for you with a low cost introductory subscription. A full year of Outdoor Life for only $6.97.

Call this number, 1-800-228-2080 and bring home the great outdoors. The action. The information. The pride . . .

Outdoor Life. I'm talking about hunting and fishing the way you like it—

 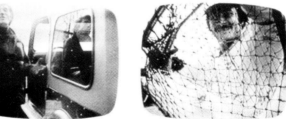

pages of tips and tactics you can use to enjoy the outdoors even more. Articles on fish and game in your neck of the woods . . . on the big ones that didn't get away and the little secrets that make it happen. Outdoor Life. It's all you need to know—from what's new in hunting equipment to where the bass are hitting big.

Lures. Boots. Boats. Fathers and sons. Adventure. Close calls and long shots.

That's the Outdoor Life for you. Equipment. Camping. Hunting. Field guides and updates and special reports on everything

from trout to turkey to white tails to mallards.

It's the tradition of caring for the wilderness, of making it on your own, through strength and smarts.

Outdoor Life. It's the man's magazine you can depend on—every month, every issue. Come with us today and get Outdoor Life's <u>Most Dangerous Game</u>— free with your paid subscription.

Call now. 1-800-228-2080 and save 53% off the $15.00 cover price. That's 40% off the regular subscription rate of $11.94. So y<u>ou</u> get 12 great issues—for just $6.97. 1-800-228-2080. For the <u>Most Dangerous Game</u>. For the great outdoors. For Outdoor Life. (MUSIC OUT)

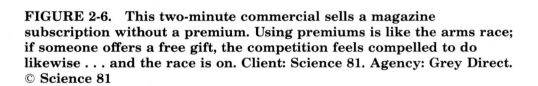

FIGURE 2-6.   This two-minute commercial sells a magazine subscription without a premium. Using premiums is like the arms race; if someone offers a free gift, the competition feels compelled to do likewise . . . and the race is on. Client: Science 81. Agency: Grey Direct.
© Science 81

(MUSIC UNDER)
ANNCR: (VO) This tiny creature

may very well make its home in your eyelashes. But where does it come from?

What makes the earth shake? Huge plates ride its molten core. But what moves them?

This is cancer created to fight cancer. Will it someday save your life?

Now the answers of science are coming—fast and fascinating. And best of all, you don't have to be a scientist to understand and enjoy it.

It's right here in a magazine called Science 81.

It's where people talk to animals—and animals answer back. Where you'll discover how life really began and where our lives are going.

Science 81. It's dreams and space and the world beneath the sea—and how they all fit together. (MUSIC STOPS)

Science 81. More than a newsmagazine, it's science straight from the source. In-depth, accurate, understandable—

It's a magazine you'll savor for its insights—and save for

its illuminating articles and stunning photography.

For the people. The discoveries. The connections.

From biogenetics to synthetic
fuel to earliest man.
(MUSIC STOPS)

Science 81. Call
800-228-2070 and join us
today. Call now and you and
your family can start enjoying
all the worlds of science . . .
in Science 81.

One year for only $12.00. A
savings of $8.00 off the cover
price. Call 800-228-2070
today.

**FIGURE 2-7.   People usually buy smokeless tobacco over the counter.
The pulling power of this commercial indicates that consumers are
ready for a change, and will accept a product directly marketed that
they are used to purchasing in stores. The commercial only mentions
the continuity program briefly. It is discussed in depth in the mailing
that arrives with the first shipment. Client: General Cigar & Tobacco
Company. Agency: Wunderman, Ricotta & Kline. © General Cigar &
Tobacco Company**

FOREMAN: (OC) If you like
smokeless tobacco, you <u>know</u>
it's got to be fresh and moist.

That's why you <u>should</u> know
about

(VO) cool, wintergreen

<u>Silver Creek</u> smokeless
tobacco.

The new, <u>Western Cut</u> brand
smokeless that's long and
shredded,

so it stays put

(OC) and the flavor keeps coming.

Silver Creek is <u>fresher</u> than you've probably ever had it before . . .

'Cause you get it <u>faster</u>, straight from the factory.

Just call us, toll-free, at 800-223-1910,

We'll rush you a "Cold-Pak" container of 6 cans of Silver Creek

with a bill for just $1.00 complete!

It will get from our cooler to your refrigerator

(VO) quicker than it normally takes most brands to reach the store.

(OC) If you like Silver Creek just tell us to keep it coming.

If you don't . . . you can throw away the bill. So call us now at 800-223-1910.

You don't know how good smokeless tobacco can be until you get it this <u>fresh</u> (BLOWS STEAM ON PRODUCT) . . .

this <u>fast.</u>

**FIGURE 2-8.   Frames 23 and 24 say it all in this continuity commercial for Harlequin Books: "So when we send you your free books, we'll also reserve a no-obligation subscription in your name. It will entitle you to six new Harlequin Romances each month. . . . "
Client: Harlequin Books. Agency: Wunderman, Ricotta & Kline. ©
Harlequin Books**

(MUSIC: ROMANTIC &
TUMULTUOUS) ANNCR:
(VO) The course of love is
seldom smooth. . . .

How did a love affair like
theirs begin? . . . And how
did it end? . . . The answer's
here . . .

locked away in books like
these four Harlequin
books—the first name in
romance.

Books so rich with the
excitement and magic of
love—

that millions are eagerly
bought every month.

Now Harlequin would like to
give away four books like
these.

Call it a gift . . . a love
token . . . as it were—

to begin a love affair of your
own. With Harlequin.

The free Harlequin sampler
will include four wonderful
romances . . .

unleasing the emotions of
love lurking in every woman's
heart.

You'll step into a world of
passion

and adventure . . .

quarrels . . . regrets . . .

and pain.

You'll meet

true-to-life people

living lives of turmoil

and larger-than-life
experiences

in faraway places.

And you'll share
their . . . treasured
memories . . . and
tenderness.

Harlequin wants to give you
four valuable books like these
because we've learned

that once you become a
Harlequin reader, it's a love
affair that can last a very long
time.

So when we send you your
free books, we'll also reserve
a no-obligation subscription in
your name.

It will entitle you to 6 new
Harlequin Romances each
month for only . . . $7.50.

That includes all handling and
shipping costs.

Every month, you can look
forward to our bringing you
hours of romance . . .

an arrangement you may
cancel whenever you wish.

But the chances are good
your love affair with Harlequin
will be a long, long one.

So to get all four books free,
here's how to order.

And begin a love affair with
Harlequin, the people who put
love into books that you can't
put down.

FIGURE 2-9.   The lead-gathering commercial is step one of a multi-phase sales program. Starrett City is a New York City apartment complex, and its commercial uses real tenants for empathy. Note the local number for viewers to call to see model apartments. Other lead-gathering commercials might have a direct mail follow-up and/or a call from a salesperson. Client: Starrett City. Agency: Rapp & Collins. © Starrett City

ANNOUNCER: (OC) In the past year,

over a thousand people have made the smart move to Starrett City.

It's almost sold out! Listen to what these people like best about living here.

1ST TENANT: (OC) It's lovely here—lots of trees, it's safe—it really works.

2ND TENANT: (OC) When I saw this place, with big rooms and parquet floors,

I said, "This is too good to be true."

3RD TENANT: (OC) I can play tennis, go swimming —it's really great.

4TH TENANT: (OC) I like walking to school—it's close to my building.

5TH TENANT: (OC) Everything

is included in the rent—gas, electricity and air-conditioning. You get the most for your money.

6TH TENANT: (OC) I can do all my shopping right outside my door.

7TH TENANT: (OC) Starrett City was nice in the commercial,

but it's even nicer now that I'm living here.

8TH TENANT: (OC) I wouldn't trade this place for anything.

ANNOUNCER: (OC) Starrett City is almost sold out.

But you can still get your chance if you call now.

ANNOUNCER: (VO) For an appointment to see model apartments,

call 265-8100. That's 265-8100.

Call now, even if you're just thinking of moving.

9TH TENANT: (OC) It's the smartest move we ever made.

FIGURE 2-10. Response television honors its heritage in this near public service spot to encourage buying through catalogs. The approach of a lead-gathering commercial offering "further information without obligation" is similar, but the follow up is more intense. Client: Direct Mail/Marketing Association. Agency: Grey Direct. © Direct Mail/Marketing Association

(MUSIC UNDER)
ANNCR: (VO) in 1872, a man named Aaron Montgomery Ward changed America.

He created something that put the whole world right in your parlor.

Children could dream of magical things. Fathers could get the bargains they wanted.

And mothers—glamour from far away.

It was the mail order catalog.

The country grew up on it. Buggies and buckets.

Trinkets and trumpets. Things to make you healthy, happy, skinny and wise.

It could all come to you in the arms of your mailman.

(SFX: CLICK OF CAMERA)
Today? Today there are thousands of ways to shop by mail. It's even more money-saving than a hundred years ago.

Shop by mail and you don't spend money driving to stores—or waste time standing in lines.

That's why you ought to call this number, 800-228-5000, for <u>DM/MA's Great Catalog Guide</u>.

It's free—a brand new listing of more than 550 catalogs that puts the world's greatest shopping right in your hands.

Shop by mail and the selection is infinitely greater. Because a world of shopping is open to you 24 hours a day.

From antiques to apples, from the down-home to the downright outrageous, you can get virtually anything

and everything delivered by mail. Straight from the source and often at tremendous savings.

Cheese direct from the barrel in Wisconsin. Tea from China. China from London.

Sweaters from Iceland. A chocolate Rolls Royce from . . . Texas, of course.

Think about it: you sit down, browse as long as you like, choose what you want and send in your order. Then it's delivered to your door. It's a terrific way to give perfect gifts, too.

Without pounding pavements or wasting gas. And you don't have to wrap or mail them. (SFX) Call this number now: 800-228-5000. The phone call is free and so is the new <u>Great Catalogue Guide</u>. There's no obligation, no cost. It's absolutely free. Get in on a great American tradition.

FIGURE 2-11.   The atmosphere and the extras at Universal City Studios, plus touches like the branding iron, add up to a solid thirty-second support commercial. It is, and should be, more of a commercial about an advertisement than a product. Client: Time-Life Books, Inc. Agency: Wunderman, Ricotta & Kline. © Time-Life Books, Inc.

(SFX: SALOON)

SPOKESMAN: Billy the Kid . . . Wyatt Earp . . .

Jesse James . . .

Can you tell the good guys from the bad guys?

This announcement in the new TV Guide introduces the Old West

from Time-Life Books . . .

America's greatest adventure . . .

get the first book, The Gunfighters, free for 10 days . . .

Just mail

this card.

And if you make this "W" into the "Bar" "W" . . .

You'll get an unframed set

of six Old West prints . . .

free with The Gunfighters . . .

Look in the TV Guide.

FIGURE 2-12.   The offer is the story in music service advertising. Here that story is told gently and atypically. Client: Columbia Record & Tape Club. Agency: Wunderman, Ricotta & Kline. © Columbia Record & Tape Club

(MUSIC UNDER)
ANNCR: (VO) So you're on your way to buy some music albums.

How much money do you have? Only a penny? You're kidding.

That won't buy a thing at the store.

But here, open this Gold Box. Just one penny buys one, two, three—keep going.

Thirteen tapes or

thirteen records of your choice, when you join the Columbia Record and Tape Club.

The New TV Guide

has this announcement ad. Look for it.

And to get a free bonus tape or record,

look for the Gold Box in the same ad.

There it is. Inside the Gold Box, write the number of any extra album you want and it's yours as a free gift.

So that's fourteen albums for one penny.

The Columbia Gold Box ad is in TV Guide.

Look for it and use the Gold Box to get an extra album.

That's a lot of music for, uh, hmm. No store offers more.

FIGURE 2-13. In this support spot for Unity Buying Service's direct mail program, the opening close-up of the perforated membership card is vital. The hero of a support commercial should be the actual thing that is being supported. Client: Unity Buying Service. Agency: McCann-Erickson March, Inc. © Unity Buying Service.

MAN: This little card from Unity Buying Service can double your buying power,

and get the things you really want, like this,

or this.

Here at Unity,

there are over ten thousand nationally advertised products at savings of up to 50%.

You save because Unity buys in huge quantities for over a million smart consumers.

Your Unity Card is coming by mail, with full details on how to start saving right away.

So watch your mail and double your buying power.

The Unity way.

3
... And Tomorrow

In speculative writing, authors get a jump on history by adapting and expanding stimulating ideas from the present and setting them in the future. This chapter is speculative; however, it is sufficiently based on today's ideas and technology that it should not be mistaken for science fiction. The only qualification I will make at the outset is that the difference between what *might* happen and what *will* happen in response television depends on two variables we can only guess at: the state of tomorrow's economy and the growth rate of interactive technology.

Assuming the worst—a crushing depression—we can always be comforted by the thought that "mail order does well in hard times." People do not make major purchases during hard times. They deny themselves, but their self-denial can serve direct marketing because the same people who won't buy in the stores will buy at home. They like the bargain appeal of many direct response products and can be swayed by the intimacy of the direct response transaction, which occurs in the security of the home, often at night, and often during periods of boredom and restlessness that the act of buying helps to relieve. Also, people will buy inexpensive, exclusive direct response products almost to reward themselves for not having made major purchases outside the home. The reasoning is the same as that of the person on a diet who orders the watercress salad in a fancy restaurant and then gobbles candies at home as a reward for being "good."

Interactive Growth Inevitable

Whatever the economic outlook, the rapid growth of interactive television seems inevitable. If the economy continues to fail, interactive television could develop as a necessity—a means for people to obtain information, services, and entertainment cheaply and efficiently. If the economy brightens, then interactive television could develop as a luxury with the marketing emphasis on fun and the good life. In any case, interactive television will grow, and most people will be able to afford it. The cost of interactive hardware for the home will drop sharply in the same way that the equipment that made interactive television possible —television and the computer—has become widely affordable. The more advertising that interactive television carries and the more personal business that can be conducted with it, the less it will cost the consumer.

The future will not remain static for response television advertising because it has so much new ground to cover. The bland sameness of most conventional commercials currently shown on television indicates that consumer advertising reached the end of its frontier some time ago. The boundaries of that frontier can be thought of in terms of the pervasive influence of commercial network television and the vast number of television households in the U.S., which peaked several years ago and shows signs of declining. In contrast, response advertising on television has grown steadily, and its boundaries, not yet clearly seen, may include the networks and their affiliates, the independently owned and operated local stations, and low-power stations, as well as cable, pay cable, and interactive pay cable stations.

It is easy to be bullish about the future of response television advertising. It is the rising star of advertising for conventional commercial television, and it is the definitive mode of advertising for interactive television. Response alone has the unique "act now, here's how" built into it, which is basic to any interactive situation. So response advertising has all bases covered regarding television present and television future. It is reasonable to expect that many more advertising agencies will become involved with direct marketing on television, or they will be forced to take a back seat to those who do.

An Extension of Today

Tomorrow's response commercials will expand all of the functions of today's response commercials. They will sell more products directly to the consumer, get more sales leads, and support more advertising. *Ultimately, anything that can be sold at any time, in any place, to anyone, and in any way can be sold through some form of response television advertising.*

Direct Response Commercials. Direct response commercials of the future will do much more than sell $9.95 record collections. When the appropriate computerized and automated distribution methods are perfected, consumers will be buying household basics through television. They won't necessarily order fruit, vegetables, and steaks sight unseen because they still might want to shop for those things in person. But they will be able to order products they don't need to examine—packaged and canned goods, for instance—and have them delivered to the door, thus saving time, trouble, and a trip to the store. The trips that they do make will be for the fun of it—for the pleasure and social experience of shopping; television direct marketing can't replace that. But it can make those trips more pleasurable by eliminating the drudgery of shopping for basics.

People will buy luxuries, as well as staples, through television. As public confidence in direct response television as a sales medium increases, more expensive items such as furniture, appliances, and other household goods will be sold directly through television. Direct marketers are going to have enough time to do more ambitious things, too. Time limits have not yet been established for commercials on cable and interactive cable television, and two minutes won't be the upper limit. Cable television is already trying "informercials" or "product programming," with no time limits, that are entirely devoted to a description of consumer goods and subsequent ordering information. (We will discuss "informercials" further on in the chapter.) There is every reason to believe that purely product shows will be a part of standard cable service in the future.

On regular commercial television, we can expect to see dramatic extensions of standard-length commercials with telephone marketing used as a creative adjunct to television. Editorial techniques, such as time compression, will permit advertisers to pack more information into their commercials. Consequently, direct marketers will have the time they need to present luxury products effectively.

Catalog sales, presently producing the largest direct marketing revenues, could readily become television transactions. It takes no leap in either technology or imagination to transform a printed catalog into a video catalog in which a customer would see the items demonstrated on the screen in contrast to printed pictures and blurbs in conventional catalogs. Customers would simply tune in a catalog channel, scan the catalog index on their TV screens, and select the items they want to see demonstrated by pushing the right buttons on a TV control box. They would also use the control box to order the items they want. At an earlier stage in interactive development, consumers would use their telephones to order.

A similar service is already available in department stores. Right now, shoppers in some stores can step up to a video catalog, push a few buttons, and see demonstrations of over 250 kitchenware products and kitchen appliances.

Lead-Gathering Commercials. Response commercials that obtain sales leads will be more efficient and personal than the ones we have today. And like tomorrow's direct response commercials, they will promote a more extensive range of products and services, including major purchase items, insurance, real estate, medical services, and educational programs. Here, too, there will be sufficient time to explain complicated propositions convincingly. And these new lead-gathering commercials and their follow-ups will be linked so strongly that they will narrow the leads-to-conversions ratio significantly.

Your prospects will be able to meet your salesperson through tomorrow's lead-generating commercials. After a commercial explains a proposition or demonstrates a product, it will be able to segue to a local dealer or representative whom your prospect can invite to make a housecall. The natural reluctance to meet strange salespeople who might take advantage of the prospect will have been overcome by the commercial's public relations function.

Support Advertising. The expansion of delayed response advertising is inevitable. This means that most of today's product advertising could become support advertising for direct marketing programs. Commercials for packaged goods will no longer simply plug their products. Although they will continue to do that, they will also tell people to look for something special printed on or inserted in the package. They will alert consumers to announcements about premiums, discounts, special offers, and free-examination privileges—all pertaining to directly marketed one-shots and continuity programs. Such commercials would, in effect, turn products on the shelf into primary advertising media. The importance of the individual product as a product would be secondary to its importance as a billboard. Of course, these commercials wouldn't dispense with the image-making and positioning functions of advertising. Mr. Whipple would still get to say, "Please don't squeeze the Charmin." But he would also tell you how to get another product when you return the free-trial certificate on the package you're not supposed to squeeze.

The Interactive Relationship

Future commercials, such as the ones I have described, may result from a newly emerging attitude toward television as something to be *used* as well as watched. A viewer's relationship with the television will become predominantly active rather than passive. The extent of this new, active relationship will depend on the number of television households that will receive cable and the number of these cable hookups that will be interactive. We do know, however, that cable has taken off like a rocket in this country; and wherever cable is installed there is an opportunity to create an interactive relationship.

Interactive hookups are able to send data from the television set at home to a broadcaster's central computer. This could develop into second-by-second, around-the-clock monitoring of what is or is not being watched. The absolute picture of audience behavior that this would provide could spell the end of the rating services as we know them. It would mean a new kind of precision in gauging audience preferences, which would give an incredible advantage to direct marketers. In the long run, the specter of Americans being monitored around the clock for any purpose raises serious questions concerning surveillance. However, such issues exceed the scope of this discussion. The issue here is simply the benefit for advertisers.

The more information marketers have about their target audiences and the more concentrated those audiences are, the more efficient their advertising can be. Even without the precision readings that interactive feedback would provide, we are profiting from the trend of today's television audience to become highly segmented. This segmentation gives us a better chance to select products and come up with offers and creative approaches that will really click with viewers who have particular interests. We already have channels devoted solely to sports, news, and movies. And it looks like the trend in specialized programming will continue, thus providing marketers with ever more self-defining audiences that will respond to advertising that fits their viewing preferences.

Technology and Time

We can also expect developments in electronic technology to lead to commercials that have more holding power and are more motivating than anything we've seen to date. The electronic medium of tape is improving every day. In many ways video tape is becoming cheaper to use than film, and it has evolved to a point where it can hold its own with the best that is being done on film. The public has yet to be exposed to the range of special effects that can be achieved on tape. When this new bag of tricks is opened for use in commercials, people will be dazzled.

Time Compression

As far as response television is concerned, one of the most promising technical developments is a technique known as *time compression*.* In time compression, commercial narration is speeded up and a computerized device is used to retain the voice's normal pitch so that the announcer doesn't sound like Alvin the Chipmunk. Narration can be boosted up to 40 percent above the normal speed of delivery without any noticeable distortion. Researchers have concluded that in some situations speed-ups of as much as 100 percent may be effective.

Direct marketers could benefit from time compression because it will help them put across more information in direct response commercials. This may be a real solution to the old battle with the clock in one- and two- minute commercials. Computerized time compression might also help make commercials more effective because the speed of delivery encourages response.

Studies of time compression published in education and psychology journals have reached some pertinent conclusions.

1. Listeners can assimilate communications at twice the normal rate of speech with virtually no loss in learning.
2. Listeners prefer communications delivered at a pace faster than normal speed.
3. The sales effect of a persuasive message does not diminish when the speed of the communication is increased.
4. Faster (radio) commercials were reported to be more interesting than commercials at normal speed.
5. Faster (radio) commercials were recalled better than normally paced commercials.

It would seem that the old-time direct response TV pitchmen understood the benefits of time compression from practical experience and used a fast-paced delivery to hold their audiences. Speed produces momentum, which fights the mind's natural inclination to wander, to daydream, to think. To get a direct response, we have to engage the mind and hold it with fast words and tightly edited visuals. When tape and the computer improve what came naturally to yesterday's pitchmen, we'll have commercials that are formidable in their holding power and persuasive-

---

*For further information on time compression, see the article on which my comments are based: James MacLachlan and Priscilla LaBarbera, "Time-Compressed TV Commercials," *Journal of Advertising Research* 18 (August 1978): pp. 11–15.

ness. Obviously, time compression and response television were made for each other.

In addition to looming developments in technology and the trend toward audience segmentation, changes in the application of media will benefit response advertisers. For one thing, we can expect to see stronger connections between different media that will favor response television. Radio, mail, print, transit, and even outdoor display advertising could effectively reinforce direct response television messages and accomplish their own specific tasks by including a telephone number or a creative element from a television commercial. Advertising that is presently used just to create awareness of a product could be adapted for response purposes.

New Time Segments

For another thing, the customary units of television time will be questioned to see if new units, better suited to response purposes, can be developed. Until now, direct response advertisers have had to make do with commercial time segments that have evolved hand in hand with traditional consumer advertising. Naturally we will continue to work in 30-, 60-, and 120-second units, but we will do so in new ways. We might try sequencing commercials so that three separate 10-second ID units followed by 30 seconds of ordering information are spread out in a two-hour program to comprise a *sequenced* direct response message. This may seem to defy common sense in media buying, but if the economics can be ironed out, it will be a way of creating a "to-be-continued" type of response commercial that could prove useful in marketing products directly. It is only one of hundreds of possibilities that deserve to be explored.

Also worth exploring are standard-length televised commercials that can be designed to carry over as commercials on the telephone. Direct marketers shouldn't always have to beat the clock. Two minutes of TV time is not enough time to sell most of what can be sold. If people are going to be asked to spend a lot of money, they need more than two minutes to make up their minds. There is no reason why a commercial has to end when two minutes are over when it can continue on the telephone as long as it takes to do the job. Sure there's no video, but an announcer's voice, music, and sound effects can all carry over to a prerecorded audiotape to continue selling what started on the screen. If you were an average woman between the ages of 18 and 34 watching a commercial about a beauty product that featured Warren Beatty, wouldn't you call the toll-free number if Warren said he would tell you more about the product if you called *him* right away? And don't you think you might buy the product if the telephone portion of Warren's message was superbly produced, exciting, innovative, and ended by connecting you with a live salesperson?

By 1980, a new category of advertising had come into being that was characterized by length. *Informercials,* or *product programming,* are program-length segments only about products. These presentations are directed to cable subscribers who wish to see them. They provide more than ample time to display and sell a greatly expanded range of products in a direct response context. And the currently low cable rates make them cost-efficient.

One of the more publicized new product programming ventures is cable TV's "Home Shopping Show." Its originator, Washburn Associates of Chicago, describes it as a

> surprisingly low-cost way to sell direct to three million households across the United States. It's an entertaining show that's built around an advertiser's product or service that's designed to show off a product's special features, benefits and uses . . . an electronic supermarket from which a shopper can buy *direct* by phone or mail . . . the kind of programming that moves people to buy.

The "Home Shopping Show" has a talk-show format with advertisers discussing their products' merits. Its creators suggest that it can be used to sell goods, offer services, develop catalog inquiries, recruit salespeople, demonstrate new products, test new concepts, enroll club members, raise funds, support retail advertising, produce new subscribers, promote franchises, generate leads, stimulate opportunity seekers, build brand awareness, and distribute "samples on demand."

Shopping at home through interactive cable television is growing in America. The year 1981 saw the introduction of a number of home shopping systems using cable television and two-way video terminals.

The Cox Broadcasting Company of Atlanta is planning to service New Orleans, Omaha, and San Diego. It expects to install about 60,000 video terminals in the next two years. The shopping service will cost about $4 monthly, and merchandise will be provided by the Fingerhut Company. Viewers will use printed catalogs with code numbers to access additional information through their terminals. Through a second and more streamlined version of the service, viewers will see the merchandise on television, order it through their televisions, and enjoy delivery in 48 hours.

Louisville, Kentucky, and St. Louis, Missouri, will have electronic home shopping through the efforts of the Storer Broadcasting Company's Atlanta cable division. The Los Angeles Times-Mirror Company is installing several hundred videotext terminals in Southern California.

Uniting Creative Efforts

Tomorrow's response television advertising could benefit from a unity of creative effort, as well as a more unified use of media and more time to sell. Today, different creative teams usually produce the various creative elements that figure into a response television campaign. In support advertising, for example, one team will come up with the product packaging and design; a second will produce the direct mail piece to be supported; a third team will create the commercial; and a fourth will produce the follow-up and collateral materials. These creative people often work out of touch with one another and have to make do with one another's work without prior collaboration. It's confused, but it's standard policy. This disjointed approach waters down the support commercial from the start because the people creating it are forced to adapt their work to preexisting materials. So great television ideas might never see the light of day simply because they do not coincide with preexisting printed material. There is no reason why an action medium like television should have to follow the lead of static media like mail and print. Mail and print may do the actual selling, but their job will be easier if the same concepts and visuals are shown to their best advantage in both the primary and secondary media. One of the things support can do is create a multiple impression. And it can do this more effectively if the support commercial is planned prior to completion of the printed material that it will support.

There can be so many steps leading to a direct marketing sale that all the steps should be tightly linked for a campaign to have maximum impact and effect. To achieve this, direct marketers should rethink the way copywriters and art directors are used. Strong concepts are often diluted because the same people do not carry through on all phases of a job. A more efficient way to work would be to have a single creative supervisor or team responsible for all of the creative materials.

Working along these lines, creative personnel would do well to favor in any other advertising the elements that work best on TV. A still shot can be taken from a moving image for dramatic use in print, but it's not always possible to take a key visual from mail or print and make it come alive on the screen. We want to move an audience with commercials that encourage a physical response; therefore, advertising that actually moves—that is, the television commercial—should determine all phases of the creative effort.

The Need to Test

Naturally, any creative point of view raises questions. But you would be hard pressed to find answers by looking at past experience. As much as the direct response industry prides itself on testing, commercials are rarely tested to discover the best creative approach. Offers are tested, prices are tested, but creative testing comes last, if at all. The results of the creative testing that has been done are not well known, and there is not enough testing from which to draw many conclusions. Testing can be expensive. As a rule, in-depth testing has been done only for costly support campaigns where considerable money must be spent on television. The creative direction of most direct response commercials produced to date, however, has been highly subjective and arrived at without the benefit of findings from focus groups or other testing procedures. (Testing and research will be discussed in chapter 5.) But as more money rides on response commercials, testing will become an economic necessity. The result of this testing will be a bank of knowledge to draw from, which will lead to more successful commercials and a medium that is more attractive to a wider range of buyers and sellers.

Response television will grow only through new ideas—and new ideas must be tested. To do so, current methods for gauging the performance of consumer advertising on television will have to be adapted or altered to suit response purposes. Entirely new methods for testing and scoring commercials will be developed along lines determined by the special considerations that figure into response advertising.

New Direct Response Genres

As response television extends its frontier, we are sure to see considerable change in both the content of individual commercials and in the creation of new contexts for commercials. Totally new commercial genres will be created. They will probably be action genres, in keeping with television becoming a thing to be *used*.

Considering direct marketing's tendency to stick with the tried and true, it's a good bet that we'll be seeing TV adaptations of action devices that have proven themselves in mail and print.

YES/NO tokens, instant sweepstakes, and transfer devices are all likely to have fresh and exciting video cognates.

Commercials will invite you straight out to participate in them. First you'll see a participatory device on the screen, and then by dialing the phone or pushing a button, you can count yourself in on an instant sweepstakes or a special offer. Whether they appear at the head or the tail of a commercial, or even somewhere in the middle, these action segments might resemble modern video games featuring simple on-screen elements that a viewer can manipulate. Today, viewers respond by using their telephones. In the long run, television will have a built-in voice-monitoring system so that words spoken directly into the television will affect the image on the screen.

Youngsters around the country already have had a preview of the participatory devices that may figure into the commercials they will see as grown-up consumers. A number of independent TV stations have invited children to send in their phone numbers for a chance to play several video games at home syndicated under the name "TV POW." The kids who are called back get a chance to play 30-seconds worth of video soccer, football, baseball, or target shooting on their own TV screens. Players make their moves by speaking into the telephone. The right moves score points that pay off in prizes. As amusing as these games are to play, they are even more fascinating as a hint of things to come.

Action-game commercials would be particularly powerful. They would hinge on motion, which in itself is motivating, and they also would ask people to make decisions faster than response advertising has ever asked before. The push would be to do it now, really now, or pass; don't think. The odds are that when the gap between reflection and action is narrowed, action will be favored.

The transfer devices people were so enthusiastic about when they first appeared in support advertising have only begun to be used effectively on television. A simple step from the commercial that asks you to check a box on a *TV Guide* insert to claim a bonus would be something we can call an *audio transfer device*— by saying a special word to the operator when you make a toll-free call to order, you get a bonus.

Video transfer devices are farther down the road. But television will reach the point where viewers will be able to use their screens like blackboards, moving around symbols by remote control. Viewers won't have to make a mark on a separate piece of paper; they will be able to check a box on their screens and remove their checks at the touch of a button.

As interesting as particular commercials that use video action devices will be, the creation of whole new genres of response commercials is going to be the most rewarding creative work we can look forward to. As it is now, only several of the many consumer advertising genres that exist have been adapted for response advertising on television. There are about two dozen basic types of television commercials, but response commercials tend to stick to straight demonstrations, which are necessary, basic, and understandable, but limiting. Among the kinds of commercials that rarely or never have been used for response purposes are: the torture test, comparison tests, symbolic demonstrations, hidden-camera interviews, man-on-the-street interviews, created personality presenters such as Josephine the Plumber and El Exijente, and elaborate production numbers with choreography, jingles, or fine animation. The consumer television genres that response does use—such as demonstration, testimonial, life-style, and slice of life—make infrequent use of the two themes that are a mainstay of consumer advertising—humor and sex.

A recent new genre is the "grafted" response commercial. This is simply an ordinary consumer spot with a response tag grafted on to it. The tag may offer a cents-off coupon, a brochure or a free sample if you call or write to the address on the screen. (For more on this see David Graham Halliday's front page article in the January 9, 1981, issue of *Backstage.)*

In one imaginative grafted commercial, an agency coupled an existing 30-second image spot for a finance company with 30 new seconds of response advertising. After the first half of the commercial runs its course, the response portion features a spokesman switching off his television as the image commercial ends. He then gives us a telephone number and reasons to call the company whose commercial we've just seen.

The response commercial for the finance company uses a familiar commercial as a starting point for a relatively fresh idea. But the reason for most grafted commercials is simply to check if an advertiser's message is getting through, and to test creative approaches—hence the appended offers, addresses, and phone numbers. It is one more indication of the respect response has gained as accountable advertising. A consumer agency that has not considered response grafting as a testing procedure has overlooked an important technique.

Unexploited genres from consumer advertising are waiting to be used. Every new adaptation will broaden the way in which direct marketers communicate through television. Considering the recent influx of general advertising talent into direct marketing, it is reasonable to assume that old, yet untried, consumer genres will be adapted quickly. For the same reason, we can also expect to see better looking response commercials.

Also awaiting us in the future are entirely new types of response commercials that will be intimate and immediate, as well as active and reactive. The new genres will elicit participation, following the lead of action devices developed for television. Direct marketers will start making commercials for people who use and interact with television, rather than for spectators, as traditional consumer advertising has done. In the next two decades, the impact of television as a communications medium will be felt more strongly than ever as it becomes evident that communication flows in two directions. Response commercials based on interaction will be one of the most important developments in the growth of television. They could even help to humanize it.

Straight Talk Wins

Television could quickly surpass even its present place of importance in the home because people have fewer opportunities to live full lives outside their homes. A catalog of grim realities is boxing the American consumer within his own four walls. Homes that once were our castles are now fortresses.

In the 1980s, Americans are working, shopping, learning, and being entertained more at home, not out of personal choice but as a substitute for living life to the fullest outside the home. Our freedom to be at large in the world and connected to one another is being replaced by the illusion that a full range of choice is ours and that we have *chosen* insularity. Commercial television, among other influences, has greatly promoted the illusion that we are engaged in life.

New technologies will make the home the shopping center of the future with television serving as the retail counter, salesperson, and cashier. Considering the negative factors that encourage the coming dominance of television, the direct marketing industry would be able to take considerable pride in itself if response commercials became more responsible and developed more of a conscience than they have ever had. Advertising reflects and helps shape life in America. A television direct marketing industry guided by consumer advocacy would be an exceptional, positive force in our lives. And it might be plain good business.

Illusions create anxiety, and a remedy for anxiety is the

truth. The best commercials are effective because they ring true. The trick is in finding the truth and using it. Honest and direct communication in a commercial medium is as desirable as it is difficult to achieve. Advertising goes into every kind of embarrassing song and dance because it is hard to be truthful about a product. Sometimes it's impossible. But more often than not, direct marketers find that straight talk wins. And in hard times when people watch their money very carefully, straight talk that reflects the truth will be a great help in selling products. People will still expect advertising to dazzle, beguile, amuse, and stop them in their tracks. But the right blend of truth and flash can do wonders for tomorrow's response advertising.

Believe in what you sell if you want to sell it well.

4
Show and Tell—The Creative Revolution

Mephistopheles identifies himself to Goethe's Faust as raw negativity. "I am the spirit that denies," he says. Negativism also plays the devil in direct marketing. There are always people in this business—account managers, even copywriters—who will tell you that "creative doesn't count." Their negativism usually follows one of two lines of reasoning. The hard-nosed among them say that you can use *any* creative execution and sell something if the product and the price are right and if you reach the right market through the appropriate media. To prove their point, they'll cite tests (usually tests of print advertising) that show how several different creative approaches for the same product and same offer performed similarly. There are also the high priests of formula—marketers whose only approach is the standard approach and who won't accept anything more. Their motto is: It worked before and it will work again.

It is difficult to argue with the gainsayers because the industry is based on results. If something made money once, who is to say it won't work again? But negativism in direct marketing comes from more than simple conservatism. It comes from being too lazy to spend the time and the energy it takes to explore new ideas. It comes from people who are so dulled from working with the same old formulas that they can't recognize anything new and promising. Pride plays a part in the negativism and so does fear—fear of risk-taking, lost profits, and losing one's job; fear of the unknown. Fear is at the heart of the negative attitudes toward creative innovation in direct response advertising, and this fear turns advertising into pap and admen into hollow men.

Granted, direct marketing would be in trouble without conservative management; however, extreme conservatism destroys creativity, which thrives on the challenge of the unknown. This can't be allowed to happen with the industry poised on the brink of becoming meaningful to the majority of American consumers. Exceptional creative work is going to help direct marketing make the leap to a larger audience, and creative people can do the exceptional only if they are not afraid of risks. You can take risks only if you are prepared to leave your job rather than compromise your creativity.

The Fight for Creativity

How do you reconcile the radically conservative part of this business with the part that needs its freedom? In purely human terms, the answer is that good creative people will fight for what they believe in. If they are not fighters, they can resign themselves to watching their talents atrophy.

For as many tests that seem to disprove the value of innovative creative advertising, there are more that prove its worth. Countering the attitude that product, price, market, and media are everything and creative is nothing is the fact that creativity is the tissue that holds these elements together—without it they would collapse. The opinion that "creative doesn't count" is a minority opinion in direct marketing. But it still haunts many writers and art directors and breaks some of them as easily as you could snap a pencil. It leads creative people away from the dangerous games they should be playing, toward the game called "playing it safe."

Response television advertising needs all the creative fire it can find. Direct marketing has never paid what top creative talent costs, so it doesn't have a long history filled with the kind of creative people who have made waves and formed policy in mainstream television advertising. But the picture is changing. With direct marketing competing more visibly than ever in the television arena, it has started to actively recruit or train the talent it needs. Some new talent is coming to direct marketing from general advertising. Some writers and art directors are making transitions within the direct marketing operations they already work for—people who once worked solely with print and direct mail are starting to do television.

Searching Out Talent

With the crying need for talent in response television advertising, it is essential to distinguish the hack from the star, the person who talks a good commercial from the person who can write one. The future is at stake. The orders you pull could be substantial or modest or you could reach or fail to reach the market you're after, depending on the creativity of your commercial. You could solve a marketing problem or leave it unsolved depending on the quality of your creative people. So whether you're staffing up or hiring a free-lancer, how do you know who will deliver?

You have to be able to judge the way people think. If you need exceptional work, you must find people who think *conceptually,* who think *visually,* whose ideas are as fine as their execution of ideas, and most important who have a feel for direct marketing.

Let's take the last things first. Direct marketing turns off a lot of people, especially creative people. It is too down-to-earth for some and has often been disparaged in the creative circles of first-class talent. But some creative talent has a lust for the hard and fast offered in direct marketing. When the lust is there, you'll know it. It's a fascination for watching orders roll in, a commitment to accountable advertising where results are in direct and attributable proportion to the creative effort. Creative people with a flair for direct marketing know *how* to get orders and inquiries and *how* to get big lifts through support. In other words, they know what the business is about.

The creative person who understands and appreciates television *and* direct marketing is a rare bird. He or she is your best bet for creating a successful commercial. But how do you assess television savvy or decide if you can develop it in a young writer or art director?

Does the writer think visually? Does the art director think like a film director? Keen visual instincts are essential for people who create TV commercials. That those instincts are often lacking is evident when you consider all the static, unimaginative commercials shown on television today. If you want to know if a person thinks visually, ask him about the movies and commercials he likes. The person who thinks with his eyes will talk about how a film is put together. He'll talk about cuts, pans, angles, and composition of shots; about art direction, casting, production values, and set design. He doesn't have an amateur's sensibility. He does more than simply like something; he knows what works and can tell you how and why it works.

This is not to say that every good creative person must think visually. Many don't, just as many "visual" people don't use words well. It's just that a heightened visual sense is essential for television, and you will meet many more people who don't have it than those who do.

Ideas Come First

Great creative people, whatever their talents, are idea people who think conceptually and wouldn't write a word or draw a line without a solid idea behind it. Creative people who do not think conceptually are, at best, the craftsmen/workhorses of the industry. They are in the unenviable position of being unable to apply their skills unless they are told what to do, yet they are essential to any operation where copy and art are produced in volume. A good workhorse can be as important as a creative superstar.

The value of the idea person is that he doesn't simply execute, he originates. That's what he's paid for. He comes up with concepts that are valuable because they have an extended lifespan and can be used in many ways, saving time and money. A solid concept can be the basis for a series of commercials. A sound idea can be used repeatedly to sell something, with applications in several media, not just one. The quality of a concept can make the difference between a commercial that runs for six months before a new one is needed and one that runs for two years. A conceptual thinker in your TV department is an investment that pays out.

In response television advertising, ideas count for more than words and pictures. The ideal creative person for TV commercials can supply all three: he has great ideas and he can tell you about them in words and pictures. The proof is in the work. You'll know if his work is good when you see his reel.

An ad agency is an idea factory, and its output is proportionate to the number of workers who think conceptually. (Apologies to those who think that advertising is too glamorous for the analogy. I use it because it focuses on output rather than ego.) In advertising you get ideas from anyone who has them, not just from the creative people. If a good idea comes from a secretary or a client or from someone in traffic, production, or account management, by all means use it. But the general availability of ideas should never diminish the importance of ideas from creative people. The difference between anyone's ideas and those from the creative department lies in the artful expression of the thought. Creative people do more than have ideas; they *communicate* ideas persuasively.

Overcoming Hang-Ups

Since creative people are paid well for what they do, it behooves those who sign the paychecks to get the most for their money, and the best. So what can management do to get the most and the best? And why do creative departments develop hang-ups—one writer who spends his days working on a novel, another with writer's block, a promising art director who starts the day at noon?

Penetrating the creative mystique can be like trying to see through a stone wall. If your people's work seems "blah" and your people seem that way too, the fault is often management's. Companies assume the personalities and values of the people at the top. And creative people can feel management's genuine attitude toward them. You can talk endlessly about developing the right atmosphere for creative work, but the atmosphere will inevitably reflect the personality of the boss or the ruling junta. Management that sincerely values creative work is more likely to get it than management that does not. It will praise and reward good work as a matter of course—a pat on the back and a decent salary being two of the things creative people need in order to work their best. They also need a sense of purpose. Advertising can seem absurd in relation to life in general. But a sense of purpose can take enough of the edge off that absurdity to allow creative people to believe in what they have to sell. If an agency is genuinely hot and feels that its work is important, the work has a better chance of really being important.

You can't fake enthusiasm for good work. If management needs something special from creative but cannot inspire great work, its creative supervisors had better be inspirational. If they are, management should leave the job to them.

Although the atmosphere that affects the quality of creative work may be a reflection of the boss's personality and is therefore abstract, there are some very tangible ways to keep ideas coming. Two important ones are provision of adequate lead time and sufficient information to do the job.

The Fear of Deadlines

An unreasonable deadline is almost certain to produce the writer's traditional nemesis, fear. People who are afraid of deadlines inevitably resort to imitation. More often than not, the imitation is approved and consequently produced. The public, who has seen it all before, responds less than enthusiastically. But there isn't too much of a stink at the agency. After all, the job got out on time. But no cigar, no breakthrough.

Some creative people need more time than others to come up with good ideas. They should have it. And if something truly exceptional is required—say an account is hanging in the balance —they should have the luxury of being able to "forget" the job for a day or two. Inspired ideas well up from the subconscious and take us by surprise. One way to tap the subconscious is to stop concentrating on the job and bypass our conscious censor of ideas. By forgetting a job, we make it unimportant, freeing it from values we would otherwise attach to it and giving it a better chance to germinate in the subconscious where original, vivid, and sincere ideas arise.

Creative people plug into the subconscious in all sorts of idiosyncratic ways. Some watch TV. Others go to the movies, take long walks, or stare into space. Their ideas may come to them in the shower or in the middle of the night. It's the payoff of all that seeming "goofing off." But in the high-pressure world of advertising where the order of the day is "more, more, faster, faster," the important step of putting a job aside is difficult to take and requires self-discipline. Creative people may avoid it altogether and be panicked into imitation if the pressure to produce is unremitting.

Orientation and Information

In addition to the time it takes to do a job well, writers and art directors need orientation and background information. Often they are told too little about what they are going to be selling. Sometimes a product comes to them without a name or a price. Sometimes information about the market or media isn't supplied. Even when background material is available, marketers may forget to share it with their creative partners. The results are time lost, a deadline fast approaching, and fear looming on the horizon.

The particulars of a job should be put on paper for distribution at the start of an assignment. This brief should contain as much pertinent information as is available on the product, competitive advertising, psychographics and demographics of the market, the media plan, budget, creative objectives, and strategies. The format doesn't matter. What matters is that it all gets written down and distributed prior to the start of work. It will serve as grist for a copywriter's subconscious mill. It will also give him or her a better picture of the market and a better chance to imagine a single, idealized customer to whom the writer can speak and achieve the one-to-one tone that is the voice of response advertising.

The Creative Spark

To get outstanding creative work, management should strike sparks in creative people. One way to do this is by making sure that the creative staff sees the best work that its competition is doing. The advertising award show annuals contain thousands of examples of work that can spark creativity in others. These books should be circulated freely rather than hidden away in the president's office.

Also begging to be seen are the Direct Mail/Marketing Association library archives of print, mail, and television commercials that have been submitted for judging in the association's competitions. This mind-jogging collection is international in scope and contains much of the best work in the business.

For TV commercial writers and art directors, movies by the masters of montage—for example, Hitchcock, Truffaut, Fuller, Sirk, Eisenstein, Lang, and Meyers—are textbooks on technique. Watching superbly produced old movies is a great way to learn the fine points of visual communication, particularly if you watch with the sound off so the technique stands out.

Experimental films and video tapes, especially the advanced work coming out of Syracuse University, have a lot to offer advertising. Shown on college campuses, at galleries and museums, and by film societies around the country, this work contains a great deal of innovative, arresting imagery that can be adapted for advertising but has yet to be seen outside the art world. Many experimental film and video tape artists are years ahead of commercial filmmakers and TV producers, and their work is a resource for ad people seeking to innovate. As Ezra Pound said, "The artist is the antenna of the race," and discoveries by artists, which might otherwise take years to reach the general public, can and do become popular through advertising—a business in which being the first to adapt an idea from another source counts almost as much as coming up with an original idea.

A late bloomer, direct response television advertising has adapted and contributed few original images to the nation's mass culture. We don't have a Bert and Harry to our credit, or the little towhead dissolving in laughter while he frolics with his puppies for Pepsi. We have nothing that even approaches the flair and diversity of the best European commercials. But keeping our eyes and our minds open can change that overnight.

The Team Approach

Being inspired by good work and digesting background material are necessary for creative people to do their jobs well. Management should encourage these things. But creative people also stimulate each other, and many times it's necessary to encourage creative people to tackle problems together. Situations often call for collaborative work. The pairing of a certain writer and art director might be necessary because a job is crying for both of their strong points. One person may be needed to balance or supplement the work of the other. You may want your juniors and newcomers to learn from your seniors, or you may have an especially thorny problem that might only be solved through a group effort. Most frequently, you team up people when you need to generate ideas in quantity.

Brainstorming and its modern-day equivalent, Synectics, are widely used to find solutions to difficult problems and produce hundreds of ideas in no time flat. From most accounts, the group-think methods have good track records. They harness imagination while they free creative associations. Their strong point is the way they encourage people to stimulate one another's thinking.

When a brainstorming group is given a problem, people are encouraged to speak up without censoring themselves or others. A leader serves to keep the atmosphere free and easy, write down everyone's ideas, set time limits for topics, and shift the focus when a topic is exhausted. One idea inevitably leads to another through cross-pollination.

Some creative people find brainstorming a little too egalitarian. They don't want to be told that a session demands that they suspend their critical judgment or that they *must* free-associate on the spot and play only one game by the rules of that game.

Brainstorming needs the illusion of freedom in order to work. Since the freedom is not absolute and members of the group have to play by the rules, some people will always hold back, preferring spontaneous self-initiated freedom to the imposed "freedom-by-the-book" of brainstorming. The quantity of ideas that brainstorming produces can't be faulted. Nor can the way it puts creative and noncreative people on an equal footing and lets them work profitably together. However, the quality of the ideas generated is another story. And after a session, participants often feel they've been squeezed dry. At a time like that, the analogy of the ad agency as an idea factory seems very appropriate, the sessions being just another way to knock out ideas on an assembly line basis. It's true that some businesses have more regard for the volume of creative output than anything else, but ultimately quality counts. It still takes the creative individual or team to perform the magic that turns people into customers.

Classical Rhetoric—A New Resource

Individuals and teams, not round tables, master the art of persuasive expression. And when you examine that art to isolate its principles, it is clear that the elements of a good commercial are the same elements of the centuries-old discipline of rhetoric.

This is particularly interesting in contrast to response advertising's need to exploit the findings of that very modern science, behaviorism.

A number of distinguished admen and influential agencies have published creative manifestos and tips for writing copy that sells. As useful as these are, the study of rhetoric is equally illuminating and possibly more so as it comes to us with a long tradition of successful application in human events by rhetoriticians of the stature of Aristotle, Cicero, Martin Luther, Edmund Burke, Danton, Disraeli, Churchill, Roosevelt, and Kennedy.

Rhetoric is the eloquent use of language to persuade, and its principles apply to television commercials as well as to oratory. Descriptions of the main elements of rhetoric—the invention and organization of arguments using figures of speech—offer valuable lessons for copywriters. For instance, rhetorical arguments are either deductive or inductive, that is, they go from the general to the specific or vice versa, which is basic in writing commercials. Following the invention of an argument, the topic under discussion is introduced with the simplest possible sentence. Then comes narration or a statement of facts, proofs, refutations, conclusions. Everything is done with brevity, clarity, and simplicity. Stale words are avoided. Specifics are preferred to abstractions. Vivid nouns and verbs are used instead of qualified language and circumlocution, and emotional appeals are saved for the very end of the argument—all sound principles for TV commercial writing.

Rhetorical figures of speech are used for special stylistic effects. They are a veritable arsenal of tricks, and many writers use them without knowing that these "tricks" have particular names and definitions that suggest ways to manipulate words and pictures in a commercial to produce a desired effect. A commercial has to move toward an inevitable conclusion, and that movement is produced by using words and pictures to make transitions from one point in a commercial to the next. Rhetorical figures of speech can suggest some of these transitions, and just about every verbal quantity has its visual cognate. There are dozens of figures of speech from alliteration to zeugma, and their definitions alone suggest tantalizing applications, especially visual applications, for those who would persuade. For example, consider possible uses for the following.

• **Antimetabole**—The repetition of words or phrases in reverse grammatical order as in "Ask not what your country can do for you. Ask instead. . . ."

- **Polysyndeton**—The repetition of conjunctions in close succession. "We have stereos *and* televisions *and* tape recorders *and* computers."
- **Metonymy**—The use of a suggestive word or phrase for what is actually meant. "I urge Congress to stop the trade in *Mail-Order Murder* by adopting a proper gun control law." Lyndon B. Johnson.
- **Erotema**—The rhetorical question. "Ladies, how often has this happened to you?"
- **Synecdoche**—Using the part for the whole (as 10 *head* for 10 *horses)*, the whole for the part, species for genus (as *headsman* for *executioner)*, genus for species, the name of the material for the thing that is made from it (as *asphalt* for *pavement)*.

Rhetoric concerns relationships between words and the effects those relationships have upon an audience. Rhetorical figures of speech are intriguing because they suggest so many possibilities for commercials. They can advance a commercial's argument and augment the basic approach of response commercials—an approach that can be summarized in that kindergarten phrase, "Show and Tell." Show an audience something that is evident, tell them about it in simple language, and they will understand. Do it rhetorically and they will respond.

The Cliché Must Go

Better commercials begin with the decision to upgrade creative standards. That decision can be expressed in a simple statement: The cliché must go! Having been creatively retarded and overly dependent upon formula, TV advertising for direct marketing has more than its share of verbal and visual clichés that weaken its impact. Many of its hackneyed words and visuals were inherited from direct mail and direct response print advertising.

When you have only two minutes or less to sell, you don't want to clutter your commercial with words that have been used so often they have lost their impact. A product or service is being shortchanged when the words describing it are stale. Get a rewrite in plain, punchy English if you're handed a script filled with tired words and phrases like the following.

Announcing. Introducing. Miracle. Magic. Hassle. Hassle-free. Extraordinary. Experience. Yours for only. That's not all. You also get. Imagine. Wouldn't you like to . . . ? Yes, that's right. Now you can. Now there is. It's everything you ever wanted and more. From the (this) to the (that). Ladies, here's how you can . . . Hi, I'm (celebrity's name). Take my advice. Take it from me. Or my name isn't (celebrity's name). You deserve it. You owe it to yourself. Much, much more.

Visual Quality

Response commercial visuals have been stagnant and in need of help for a long time. Too many response commercials have been cranked out on shoestring budgets without regard for quality or polish. The worst thing about them is that they are relatively static. No pains are taken to build in motion, even though motion is necessary to carry the audience with the momentum produced through careful shooting and editing.

Talking heads drone on, and products just sit on the screen without any action to keep the eye interested. Most shots are simple medium shots, without even a slow zoom in or out. Extreme close-ups, wide-angle shots, crane shots, and telephoto shots are avoided. You rarely see tracking shots and effective matching shots in most response television advertising. The kind of good editing that keeps the eye hopping is seen too infrequently. Special optical effects are handled amateurishly, and lighting, casting, and set design are frequently substandard. Yet response television advertising wants to reach a larger audience of non-mail-order buyers. It cannot unless its commercials can hold their own with the best in the business.

Visual quality in a commercial depends on how the commercial was shot and edited. A few simple rules of thumb for judgment in these areas are:

1. A scene or an image must have good lighting and composition.
2. Quality stands in direct proportion to the number of camera angles and camera set ups a director considers before shooting. (A conscientious director will explore several ways to do each shot and go to the trouble of setting up the camera in a new position if a shot calls for it.)
3. "One-take" directors are to be avoided.
4. Editing is critical. The more care taken with editing, the better the commercial. Precise synchronization of picture and sound is essential and is achieved through editing. Often, the commercial that is heavily edited is better than the one that is not because "edits" provide transitions from image to image, thereby holding the viewer's interest.

Producing a Commercial

Unfortunately, many direct marketing people still feel uncomfortable doing commercials. Sometimes the problem is a simple as a writer not knowing the correct format for a script. Sometimes lack of familiarity with TV commercial production causes hesitancy. For all who could benefit from a review of what goes into producing a commercial, the next few pages will take you from start to finish.

It Starts with an Idea

A commercial starts as an idea—a visual idea that will satisfy both a marketing objective and a creative strategy based on a product, the market, the media, and the competitive picture. Commercials miss their marks when they don't live up to their ideas. To narrow the gap between idea and execution, every part of the commercial and its production should be examined separately to assure that it supports the main idea.

Creative people who come up with ideas must remember that their scripts and storyboards will be subject to interpretation at every stage of production. Concepts will not be lost if the scripts and storyboards are tight and indicate precisely everything that should be seen and heard. Every image, action, angle, expression, and effect should be in writing to provide a basis for discussion in preproduction meetings.

The Script

Scripts are usually written in two columns with all of the visuals broken out and numbered on the left, the audio on the right. When a job is very complex, a script might have as many as five columns headed: video, opticals, sound effects, music, and voice. (A well-prepared script will often include a short summary of the general action, a casting brief, and production notes.) Abbreviations are used to keep directions short and simple. About two dozen abbreviations for directions are used regularly, and some writers simply make up their own as needed. The following is an adequate basic glossary.

VIDEO	AUDIO
POV—point of view	VO—voice-over
CUT—edit in next visual immediately	SYNCH—synchronized sound
DISS—dissolve	SFX—sound effect
RIP—ripple effect	ANNCR—announcer
EXT—exterior	MUSIC UP—music swells
INT—interior	MUSIC UNDER—music in background

PAN—camera moves across

TRACK—camera moves with
      action

ZOOM—stationary lens moves
      in or out

FADE—(either in or out)

ECU—extreme close-up

CU—close-up

MED or MS—medium shot

MASTER—master shot taking
        in entire scene

L.S.—long shot

W. ANG—wide-angle shot

TEL. S.—telephoto shot

SLOMO—slow motion

STOPMO—stop motion

FREEZE—freeze frame

2-SHOT—two people
      frame

MATCHING SHOT—major elements in next
            visual correspond to
            elements in previous visual

WIPE—next frame pushes off
      present frame

S.S.—split screen

SUPER—superimpose

BKGRND—background

FRGRND—foreground

MUSIC OUT—music stops

Formats for scripts are simple, but what goes into them is more difficult. Good scripting calls for words and ideas with visual potential. A major approach in scripting is to go from the small to the large or vice versa, verbally and visually. A commercial like this will show and tell how "the world comes alive once a week, every week in *Newsweek,*" or how "over a century of craftsmanship is reflected in every Wittnauer watch." They can show you the world implied in a single issue of a magazine or a century of history focused in one little product because time, history, distance, and matter can be expanded or contracted as needed.

Another important approach in writing effective commercials is to make the ordinary, extraordinary and the unusual commonplace. This kind of switch is an almost certain attention-getter and can be used advantageously to express product attributes and consumer benefits. Commercials using this approach transform reality by characterizing people, objects, or attitudes according to their contrary attributes, by transforming them to their opposites and then drawing extravagant parallels. Thus, a baggage handler is shown as gorilla slamming around a suitcase in a cage to prove that the product is durable.

Commercials that succeed in going from the general to the specific and in making the ordinary seem extraordinary are usually written so that contrasting elements are combined with memorable effect. A good writer is able to tie several ideas into one neat package. He must also create smooth and reasonable transitions from one point to the next so the viewer will accept the commercial's basic premise and the need to order the product. The right combinations and transitions are particularly important if a commercial is funny or surrealistic. You will ultimately have to bring people back to earth to get them to dial that 800 number.

Straight Talk and Demonstration

Because the commercial does the actual selling in direct response, writers must be able to create unique and pointed demonstrations. Finding new ways to demonstrate is difficult, but the problem becomes simpler when you anchor a commercial in straight talk. Straight talk, not to be confused with the pitchman's amazing slight-of-mouth, is plain and direct language that is effective because it is simple and condensed. A budding writer should study prose stylists like Ernest Hemingway, Dashiell Hammett, and Charles Bukowski. They literally wrote the book on the short, punchy sentence that telegraphs its meaning like an electric shock.

People who order merchandise through television want to know exactly what they are getting and possibly getting into. They want to know why they should "act now" as the commercials urge. Straight talk gets right to the point with no extraneous words. It is best used to demonstrate and explain—*why* a price is low, *why* such an offer can be made, *what* you are getting for your money. If the visuals are bright and proud, straight talk is sometimes all that it takes to turn interest into action.

Creating the Storyboard

Storyboards should be prepared after a script is written and approved. They should be precise because they will be a blueprint for everyone making the commercial. The storyboard should follow the script closely, and because it is made of drawings, it will express what is wanted on screen better than the written word. The more the storyboard looks like what you want, the more likely you'll get exactly what you want. When you are preparing the storyboard, you can pin down details in costuming, actors' expressions and gestures, color schemes, lighting effects, the composition of shots, and dozens of other details that the script only indicates.

An alternative to a storyboard is a *key-frame drawing;* it doesn't show the complete commercial but presents a scene from the commercial that best expresses the concept and the main action. Key frames are used for economy's sake, when a proposed execution is particularly clear and simple, or when many ideas are being presented. Sometimes it only takes one key frame to explain a commercial; sometimes it takes two or three. But whether you are using storyboards or key frames, formal presentations call for well-drawn, well-mounted materials. Because these visual aids deserve more than a cursory glance, copies should be handed out after the commercial is presented.

The Bidding Procedure

When a storyboard has been approved, several independent producers are invited to bid on the commercial. Price and quality are equally important. A producer's strong points will be evident on his or her reel. You will want to find a producer who specializes in the treatment your commercial calls for—animation, a documentary approach, spectacle, or outstanding work with actors, for example. Several independent production companies may say that they specialize in direct response, but be wary of such claims. Their so-called specialization may consist of a number of "down-and-dirty" quickies on tiny budgets. Find a producer who is equal to the job the storyboard requires and, happily, can improve on it. (Producers should submit estimates on something similar to the AICP Studio Cost Summary form in Appendix D.

Like everyone else in advertising, producers rest on their laurels and put their best footage forward. However, some of the people responsible for the commercials on demo reels may no longer work with the producer. It's best to ask who will shoot, light, design, and edit your job, and if their work is on the demo reel. If the crew looks like it is going to be the right one and the bid is reasonable, it's time to proceed.

Production Ground Rules

The ground rules for a good production are the same as those for coming up with a good script. Give the producer the time and the materials he needs to do his job well. If he is going to work with mock-ups or still photographs that you will supply, make sure he gets them when he says he needs them. If a location has to be chosen, give him time to find it. If casting could prove a problem, allow for the time it takes to find the right talent.

Time can work for or against you, and time is well spent in pre- and post-production because it saves you money in the long run and helps you get the quality you want. Legwork, research, and careful planning before the cameras roll costs little enough and gets you more for your money during the shoot. Your producer has to make the most of your budget. So keep in mind that the biggest part of your budget goes for salaries, talent payments, and rental fees for equipment and studio facilities. Likewise, by working closely with your producer during pre- and post-production, you will be making the most out of him.

A producer will handle every technical detail of a production. He will assemble the cast and crew and arrange for salaries and talent payments. He will obtain props, costumes, materials, and equipment and will negotiate the use of locations, set construction, and reservation of studio time. Your producer will also arrange for all the services your commercial needs, such as animation, optical and other special effects, stock footage or stock music, original music, choreography, lab work, recording, and editing. He will stick with your commercial through all phases of production: sound recording, shooting, editing, mixing, the rough cut, answer print, and dubs.

The producer's judgment is particularly important in his choice of people. He will usually choose the cameraman, soundman, lighting engineer, technicians, script girl, set designer, costumer, make-up artist, and director (if the producer is not directing). The choice of director is critical. Although the director is not responsible for the commercial's concept or content, he or she is responsible for the way it looks, just as an art director would be responsible for the look of a print ad. You want a perfectionist-expediter in the director's chair, not someone who has only one of those qualities.

You will also want perfect talent for the job. Finding it is an art and, with luck, your producer has mastered the art of casting. Fine actors and sharply defined character types are best obtained through the leading casting agencies. Response advertising needs the best actors it can get; it has skimped on talent too long. You need more than a face to convince people to "call now"; you need trained actors who can bring words to life persuasively. Actors humanize commercials by creating that one-to-one tone you need.

Attend enough casting sessions and you'll discover that a good actor is hard to find. It will help if you have already given your producer a written description of the talent your commercial requires, specifying age, physical qualities, and character type. Still, casting may take time. You may see scores of people before you find the right actor. You may even have to pay a premium for high-caliber talent. It's not unusual for accomplished actors to ask for double scale, and they're often worth the price.

Stock Music and Footage

If you can afford it, it is also worth paying for the perfect music, stock photos, and stock footage. These may or may not be inexpensive depending on the source but, most often, the cheaper the price the poorer the quality. Sometimes fees for stock materials are negotiable. If you do enough digging, you may get a bargain from a private copyright holder. You may even find what you want in the public domain. If your commercial needs a number of very specific photographs, you might do well to hire a photographer and have him stage and shoot the photos rather than pay a stock house for pictures that are often expensive and inadequate. If you want something specific, never assume that perfect stock photos, footage, or music will be available. Often material you think would be abundant just can't be found, and the commercial has to be compromised or scrapped.

Stock music can be inexpensive—and terrible. You might discover that you can avoid stock music altogether and score your commercial for less than you'd imagine. Remember, the masterworks are in the public domain. However, fine composers and musicians are willing to work for a reasonable price, and your producer should be able to find them.

There aren't many bargains in stock footage. Only a few companies have made a real business out of it, and you may have to pay a research fee just to see what they have. Hollywood studios rarely make footage from their movies available for commercials. When they do, the price is usually prohibitive. The only inexpensive sources of stock footage are some of the companies that market 16-millimeter prints of old movies, newsreels, and cartoons, much of which they purchased when the prints became public domain. Most of it is black and white. The poor quality of this material may make it inadequate for your needs.

The Importance of Motion

Some comments on filming and editing in general are in order. Movies have to move and so do commercials. Motion in a commercial helps to produce a direct response because it keeps the viewer's attention glued to the narrative flow, which ends with an invitation to order. Your commercial's chance to keep the audience interested increases in direct proportion to the amount of action it incorporates.

Whenever possible, a sequence should have action built into it, be in an actor's movements, pure camera action like a tracking shot, or action produced by editing. The cumulative effect of the individual sequences should be a sense of forward motion that will produce a sympathetic forward motion in the viewer. Don't settle for a static commercial if you can build motion into it, unless you are using lack of motion for impact. If you're showing a product, emphasize its features and functions as you would in a direct mail brochure, but bullet them with film action. Show as much as you can in motion.

If you are working with still photos, the need for motion is critical. You can achieve motion by shooting your stills on an animation stand where the camera can move interpretively. You'll want to use large color transparencies or color prints. Because 35-millimeter slides may be too small for the camera to move on, you may want to enlarge them.

When you use type directly or superimpose it, explore ways it can be used to enhance motion, to augment visuals rather than obscure them, or to have impact by itself. Be imaginative with type, and don't use a crawl if there is a better way to present typeset information.

When you think about motion in your commercial, think in terms of time. *Motion is time* in film and tape, and by using motion you can create an illusion of time—the time you need to convince people to *do it now*. A commercial's comprehensive sense of time is made up of the cuts and dissolves you edit into it. Cuts usually represent fractions of seconds; dissolves can stand for the passage of minutes or centuries. There are exceptions, of course. A simple cut from someone saying "Merry Christmas" to the same person saying "and Happy New Year" in *Citizen Kane* represents a leap of more than a decade.

Good editing creates a context of time for a commercial. It also brings out a commercial's logic, rhetoric, and structure and limits the viewer's inclination to see your commercial in his own light. The eye registers images in fractions of seconds, which is sometimes all it takes to make a persuasive impression. But when you want a direct response, the eye has to be told what it is seeing. This is achieved through editing by linking pictures to words or sounds that make the meaning of those pictures specific.

Never settle for lazy editing. The more creatively ambitious you become, the greater the demands you'll place on editing, and you will want to plan on paper, in advance, every second. The well-shot, well-edited commercial can contain several layers of meaning. One layer may be purely visual or musical, appealing to the emotions. Another layer should be narrative/descriptive, addressed to the viewer's conscious logic and reason. It may be that commercials with distinct layers of meaning will be more likely to engage the whole mind—the right and left hemispheres of the brain that research indicates are involved with emotion and analysis, respectively. We may actually discover that a commercial will produce more responses if it is shot and edited with sufficient precision to engage both sides of the brain simultaneously. This is another one of those unknowns on the response frontier that await exploration.

Film or Tape—The Great Debate

A less academic question that frequently comes up is which medium to use: film or tape? Everyone has a favorite. Most producers are prejudiced in favor of one or the other because of their personal experience with these media. Both have advantages and disadvantages that are not always presented objectively. Trade papers add to the confusion. In one issue they'll hype film, in another, tape. It's hard to get the facts straight.

The decision to use film or tape is a decision for the person paying the bills. It should be based on the demands of time, budget, and most important, *on the particular visual quality the commercial calls for!*

Film— A Glorious Antique

Film and tape are different and they look different. Film is a glorious antique capable of many nuances and unique effects. It has been around for nearly a century and is a highly developed medium with a long tradition from which to draw. The characteristic distinguishing film from tape is the sense of depth it conveys. In film, depth is a delicate softness, an almost imperceptible blurring of the outlines within a frame. It's there because of a grain tape doesn't have. Filmmakers who have mastered their equipment enhance this special sense of depth, creating what has come to be known as the quality look of film. This beautiful look is unmatched for creating a mood of timelessness in a commercial, a sense of substance and significance. The richness of film is unmistakable. It remains the medium to use if the commercial is telling a quality story in a traditional way. Use film to link eternal verities to a product or service, or use it for institutional promotions.

If you work with film, you will have to decide whether to use 35-mm or 16-mm stock. To date, more direct response commercials have been shot in 16 mm than in the bigger and more costly 35 mm, which is commonly used for feature films. This makes sense since the right lenses and right 16-mm stock will produce results that are indistinguishable from 35-mm footage. Tests show that consumers do not differentiate between versions of the same commercial shot in 16 mm or 35 mm.

The commercial itself should determine which size stock to use, just as the quality you're looking for should govern your decision to use film or tape. For technical reasons, sharp free-flowing animation is more easily achieved when you use 35-mm film. Furthermore, if 16-mm film is carelessly shot and must be enlarged to 35 mm, it can look coarse and grainy. Nevertheless, it is usually more than adequate for all live action.

Tape—Some Advantages

As communications industries become increasingly committed to video technology, it seems that the days of film are numbered. Film is still the quality medium, but tape has come into its own.

It used to be that taped commercials looked flat, harsh, dimensionless, and uninteresting. The lighting for tape was generally slapdash and produced a flat, characterless look that lacked quality and dimension. For a long time, the single creative advantage of tape was that people regarded what they saw on tape as being more real and immediate than film, probably because a taped commercial looks similar to live, on-the-spot TV coverage.

Tape has come a long way in a short time. Its technology and the people using it have improved so much since the flat old days that tape is succeeding in turning film into a functional antique.

The biggest plus for tape is still the sense of immediacy it conveys. If you are creating a "happening now" situation, what you show on tape will look more like "now" than the same situation on film. Further advantages of tape are the brilliant colors it captures and the sharpness of tape images. The images are so sharp that, even when the commercial is shot on film, telephone number and address tags are frequently taped for greater clarity. Tape commercials are better than ever because of the more frequent use of the excellent new one-inch C-format tape stocks available, the more common and skillful use of computerized editing, and the growing craftsmanship among video technicians.

Tape commercials needn't be flat anymore and frequently aren't. When a scene is properly lit, tape has depth, but it is different from the depth of film. With tape there is no subtle blurring of the image outline; depth is a matter of hard-edged planes in perspective. Tape conveys an effective and fitting sense of depth for these hard-edged times that is as impressive as film depth, though different.

Bad lighting probably accounts for more unattractive-looking commercials on tape *and* film than anything else. This has been a particularly common problem since film-lighting techniques should be used for tape, but people using tape often do not take the equivalent amount of trouble to use proper lighting. This underscores the real issue in deciding whether to use film or tape: Who will be using the film or the tape? The people shooting the commercial make it good or bad, not just the medium chosen and the equipment used. Today there are probably fewer real craftsmen working with tape than with film, but this will change as people become more familiar with tape and the range of special optical effects it can achieve.

The choice to go with tape is often made for practical reasons alone. Creative arguments that tape is not aesthetically right for a certain commercial are often overlooked because tape is supposed to be fast and inexpensive. Tape may be faster and cheaper than film, depending on what the job calls for, but this is not universally true. Given the nature of a commercial and the people making it, a commercial on film can end up costing less than the same job done on tape.

Nevertheless, tape has undeniable advantages—it's the instant playback medium. You don't have to wait for the dailies to come back from the laboratory. Editing in the camera is also easier when you're using tape. But faster and easier do not necessarily make a good commercial. Good work comes from painstaking care. If you select tape because it's faster, cheaper, and easier, your commercial may end up looking fast, cheap, and easy. Tape is today's medium because it is compatible with the electronic medium of television. But more good-looking commercials are still being done on film rather than tape because people know more about film and can do more with it. You can even get instant playback when you're shooting with film if you rig a tape camera piggyback to the movie camera.

The Cost Consideration

Tape has moved as far and as fast as it has largely because of its price advantage over film. In the icily practical world of advertising, price is the determining factor in what gets produced and how. Being new to TV, direct marketers are particularly sensitive and uncertain about production costs. Not knowing what they can get for their money, fledglings in TV direct marketing sometimes fail to recognize inflated budgets or they turn down bids that are reasonable. They may accept less than they paid for or expect more than they can afford. The only way to cut through the confusion is to question many producers about quality and price and to shop around.

Costs are confusing. Most fees are negotiable. There is usually a gilt-edged and a bargain-basement way of doing the same commercial. There are no hard fast rules about costs. One production company might bid a storyboard at $3,000 while another will ask $30,000 for the same job. Your needs and your judgment will determine who gets the job. You get what you pay for, and you pay for talent and experience. More often than not, a low-budget job looks low budget and this is no way to reach a larger audience.

Nevertheless, many direct marketers have only small budgets to work with, so they have to think and work twice as hard as other marketers to stretch their money and still get the quality they need. The more you know about TV commercial production and the more talent and suppliers you are acquainted with, the further your money will go.

Union vs. Nonunion

Right now, the big factor in determining what it costs to make a commercial is whether the job is going be "union" or "nonunion." A job produced with the blessings of the various trade unions involved in TV commercial production requires the payment of union-scale wages and high overtime, if necessary, to as many people as the union designates the job requires. Talent may be paid no less than scale, and there may be costly residuals to pay as well. Costs and corners are cut on nonunion jobs. Crews are usually smaller and may be paid less than union wages. Talent is "bought out," paid once and once only, so residuals and sometimes even union scale need not be paid.

The advantages of the nonunion route for the direct marketer with a limited budget are obvious. But every direct marketer cannot take the advantage of this option because he or his agency may be signators of union contracts, which limit them to certain procedures. Still, most direct response commercials by small entrepreneurs are nonunion because these businesspeople are neither union contract signators nor do they have a vested interest in the broadcast communications industry where union pressure could be brought to bear against them.

Doing a nonunion commercial is not a matter of getting away with something, because the whole union-nonunion issue is gray. Unions will sometimes negotiate fees if they are satisfied that there just isn't enough money available to go the straight union route.

Being able to go nonunion is something that gives the small direct marketer some degree of parity with his wealthier counterpart. But there are upper and lower rungs on the nonunion ladder. For every really talented nonunion producer there are many more *schlockmeisters*. Study a producer's reel carefully before you decide to give him your job and never think that your commercial will look any better than what you've seen on the reel. Chances are it won't even look as good.

Local independent TV studios also produce commercials. They will assign you a producer/director, get the talent you need, and tape your commercial quickly and inexpensively. Quite a few response commercials are shot this way, but it is rarely quality work. TV studios might sandwich your commercial between programs when their cameras are free. Commercials shot this way look rushed. Working like this may be expedient. It may be all you can afford to determine if an idea will work on television. If a cheap commercial works, you would do well to think of that commercial as a test and go ahead with a more polished production. TV commercials, like direct mail and direct response print ads, have a lot to gain from subsequent refinements.

Stretching your imagination about how to get things done creatively will help you to stretch your budget. But ideas and budgets only stretch so far. The best on-camera talent is inevitably union talent; the same applies to the people behind the cameras. Real quality costs money and has a union label.

No Easy Answers

This chapter is as close as response television ever comes to "how-to" advice. Direct marketing literature is filled with "how-tos": "How to write sure-fire copy that sells," "100 proven ways to do this or that," or "The basic steps to guarantee creative interaction." More often than not the pundits have been right, and there's the rub. They *have* been right. But what *has* worked can retard innovation when it becomes dogma.

The indispensable element in creativity is the unknown—the blank sheet of paper, the question looking for an answer. Most of the "how-tos" in the business advocate imitation. They prefer the formula to innovation, which implies the unknown. A successful formula may mean only that an approach works well enough with a portion of the total audience to make advertising profitable. It may be that the same formula repels a large portion of that audience.

It is not the prime business of modern direct marketing to talk to only the country's relative minority of confirmed mail-order buyers. We know how to speak their language already. We want the non-mail-order buyers, and we have to learn how to speak theirs. Formulas do not show us how to do that, so we have downplayed the "proven-method" approach in favor of the principle that creative people have to find their own way once they know the business of direct marketing. *Finding new ways to reach new customers is the creative revolution in response television, and innovation is the impetus for that revolution.* At present, the revolution hinges on the crossover of styles, techniques, and production values from general advertising to direct marketing. The results have been invigorating. Beyond this phase is the point where direct marketing develops its own new language for television.

When you consider that response advertising affects behavior and that response rates are rough measures of behavior, it is reasonable to assume that subsequent phases of our creative revolution will rely more heavily on the findings of behavioral science. This doesn't mean that we are going to come up with magic formulas that will make people respond in spite of their better judgment. It means that direct marketing's creative people will find out how to involve viewers in commercials by cashing in on the dynamics of social conditioning, using behavioral phenomena, such as the Zeigarnick effect, which makes the observer a participant by presenting incomplete material which the viewer makes complete, as in: "You can take Salem out of the country, but. . . ."

People can be encouraged to supply missing pieces in advertising, and a direct physical response can be a missing piece as much as a thought. A commercial can cash in on preconditioning by incorporating any of the innumerable words, phrases, thoughts, sounds, and images that are so familiar to us that, when severed, beg completion. A vast reservoir of this material is waiting for creative application: the first three notes of the opening bar of Beethoven's Fifth Symphony will demand the fourth note from the listener if it is not played. A viewer would be hard pressed not to add a third X to two waiting in a row in tic tac toe. If I say "The Lone Ranger and . . . ," you think Tonto. And on and on.

This is only a glimmering of what could lead to a new

direction in response television advertising once it has merged with mainstream television advertising. This new direction eludes description because creative people are just starting to wrestle with essential unknowns that offer the resistance required for breakthroughs. But the search for unknowns to push against begins by asking why people either participate in response advertising or turn off to it.

A viewer who responds to a commercial is completing a circuit; therefore, when the commercial is planned, he should be seen as a component of the circuit and not as something outside it. We do less than our job calls for if we think we can lead people down the garden path. What is in the minds of our audience is part of the path itself, and we can only get to the end of it, to the response, if we create commercials that capitalize on predispositions to participate.

Direct marketing will continue to reach more qualified markets more efficiently. It will become more meaningful to more consumers every year. But it is going to take the creative revolution that is happening now to bring about dramatic shifts in these areas. The future scope of direct marketing depends on creative breakthroughs in television. One breakthrough will be worth a score of average commercials.

5
Research—Testing and Scoring Response Commercials

Television commercial research basically asks how well a commercial is likely to perform and why. In a sense, orders and inquiries from direct response commercials are research findings themselves because they are clear measures of a commercial's performance. Accountable advertising answers the questions it raises; however, those answers can come too late to determine the form and content of the advertising at issue. It's a lot better to copy test early in the game in order to evaluate and improve your commercial. Nevertheless, commercials are tested infrequently in today's response television; most frequently tested are offers, price, marketing strategies, and positioning. Creative executions are tested least.

Old-timers in the business tend to act on gut instincts and forget about testing for television. Even progressive industry professionals, who work with budgets so big that testing is mandatory, often pay little more than lip service to pretesting commercials. I remember one slip of the lip by a top direct marketing executive that summed up the whole unspoken attitude about pretesting. "We'll review all of the creative work we've done," he said, "and then we'll arrive at our decision subjectively . . . I, I mean *objectively.*"

He was right the first time as far as his feelings were concerned. Personal taste and opinion have been the guiding light in advertising from the start. Even where research is undertaken, the criteria for testing and the interpretation of test results are often highly subjective. But degrees of subjectivity will always be present in advertising. People are subjective, and subjectivity is a kind of anarchic truth. So the question is not how to eliminate subjectivity, but how to work with reasonable degrees of subjectivity from both consumers and advertisers.

Research and testing had to fight long and hard to gain acceptance in consumer advertising where they have proven their worth. The same battle is now being fought in direct marketing. And money is turning the tide in favor of research. With more money than ever going into commercial production and TV time, advertisers want to make every dollar count. They want protection, insurance. Consequently, the big testing in response television has been conducted where the most money has been spent—in campaigns supporting costly mass mailings and *TV Guide*/Sunday paper announcements.

That testing occurs where the big money is shouldn't discourage the small entrepreneur from testing. He can do a great deal with a modest test budget. What's important is that any direct marketer using television should develop an open, objective, and questioning attitude and not mistake copy testing for something it isn't—a tyranny of numbers and statistics aloof from interpretation. Research and testing cannot replace judgment; they aid judgment. They cannot answer questions about how advertising will perform ultimately, but they can help you reach your own conclusions about those questions.

Copy-Testing Methods

The available methods of copy testing television response commercials have evolved from and are related to general advertising. Direct marketers must either adapt these methods for their own purposes or create new techniques that are better suited to evaluating response television. Of the methods we have today, focus-group interviews and in-depth personal interviews are valuable because they can be structured openly enough to get feedback that lets the market literally write its own response commerical.

The principal copy-testing methods now in use evaluate whether a commercial holds the viewer's attention and communicates its information. Only some methods are concerned with persuasion and, here, persuasiveness is thought of in terms of what the consumer *might* do or says he is going to do rather than if he acted on the spot, which is what the direct marketer wants to know. No present copy-testing method thoroughly examines whether or not a commercial produces a direct response. Today's testing systems get closer to consumer attitudes than consumer behavior and, when they are used to evaluate a direct response commercial, the absence of motivational measurements must be taken into account.

This is not to say that consumer TV copy-testing methods are without value. One of the best-known methods (although it is currently under fire as being inadequate for general advertising, which has long revered it) is Burke Marketing Research's Day-After Recall System, which is designed to find out how well a commercial is remembered 24 hours after viewing. A version of this measure may be of value for TV support campaigns of direct mail and direct response print, but Burke doesn't measure persuasiveness, let alone motivation. This testing system can tell us if a commercial sticks in the mind, but it can't tell us how a commercial acts upon the mind to affect behavior.

General advertising copy-testing methods use two principal testing environments. They are either "on-the-air" systems or "in-theater" invited viewing environments (in which respondents either know or do not know that they are reacting to commercials).

On-the-air systems test recall, and all of them choose viewers through random telephone calls. Their strength is that they study the impression a commercial makes in a natural environment—the home. On-air systems include Burke, Gallup & Robinson's Total Prime Time, In-View, and Single Show Surveys; the Mapes and Ross Recall System; and the Sherman Group's BUY Test.

In-theater systems—such as McCollum-Spielman's AC/T, ASI, and ARS—try to simulate natural exposure to television commercials. Audiences are recruited for group viewing of "programs," but their reactions to commercials within the programs are actually being studied. These services are capable of screening for target prospects. They measure key areas such as attention, communication, persuasion, and recall; and they can obtain diagnostic information. They let advertisers get a reading on rough-test commercials which is not possible with traditional on-the-air systems.

The so-called "forced-exposure" in-theater systems can also present rough commercials to target samples. But unlike methods used in other in-theater systems, respondents are told that they have been chosen to evaluate commercials. Among these systems are Tele-Research and FCB's FOCUS and Communications & Attitude Change Study. They offer no real method of studying a commercial's ability to gain attention.

As you can imagine, some tests are expensive, particularly if you need to interview a large sample of people, if your target audience is difficult to isolate, or if testing needs to be done in many geographic regions. But ways can be found to test if the will to test is there. Anyone can test who is willing to find the market and ask it questions.

When you test, have clear questions in mind. For instance, test major copy points. Study demographics and psychographics prior to testing and stick with the same methods of measurement in both pre- and post-testing. Test offers, formats, strategies, positioning, and creative executions singly. Don't expect a test of whether people will buy a certain product through direct response television to tell you who is going to buy that product or what your creative approach should be.

Translating the Findings

The value of research is in interpretation, not in data reduced to generalizations, numbers, and yes-no answers. Direct marketers come as close as any media user can to making a face-to-face sale. And considering the direct marketer's particular bent toward the personal approach, it stands to reason that he is uniquely suited to test and translate research findings into advertising that communicates and motivates. What's more, because direct marketers are so perceptive and personal in their approach to the consumer, they can benefit not only from test results but also from participating in tests in order to refine what is being tested *as the feedback occurs*. Nothing is more sobering or valuable than meeting your market face to face and adjusting your work to that market.

An exercise in copy testing by Wunderman, Ricotta & Kline for the General Cigar & Tobacco Company is a good example of how testing can be used creatively and on the spot to create a winning commerical. Wunderman's testing was highly uncommon in direct response, and the outcome of the test opens the frontier even wider. The agency was trying to find out if a mass market consumable previously sold only over the counter could be sold direct through television. The results of the test were affirmative, and a review of the test is valuable for everyone who is willing to work with the information that a target audience sample can reveal.

To conduct the test, an account supervisor and copywriter went to Oklahoma City where focus groups were being tested for their reactions to a new brand of smokeless tobacco. The agency people brought along a rough, taped commercial that featured an actor in no particular setting introducing the product and telling how to get it through television. The actor and a video cameraman also went to Oklahoma because, after each time a battery of focus groups would be exposed to the commercial, it was to be reshot according to their comments and presented to different focus groups the next day for further refinements. The original commercial had been created without the benefit of this kind of market input.

The commercial was shown to three focus groups per evening for three consecutive evenings with about 15 people in each group. Their comments to predetermined questions were carefully noted, and the commercial was rewritten twice on the basis of those comments.

The first evening's groups didn't want to buy the product through television. They didn't believe that it would be fresh when they got it, they thought that it would take too long to reach them, and they didn't trust direct response commercials in general.

The first rewrite produced a commercial that told people they would get the product faster through television than any other way. Their satisfaction was guaranteed because they were promised that they could have their money back (a one-dollar qualifier) if they were not satisfied.

The second evening's focus groups responded well to the new commercial with most but not all of those interviewed expressing strong interest in getting the product via television. Comments from the first and second evening's groups, particularly about the qualities of the product and its packaging, led to further refinements of the direct delivery story. When the last groups saw the final version of the commercial, their enthusiasm was virtually unanimous. Some of the people even quoted the telephone number without prompting.

Copy testing combined in this way with copywriting resulted in a total shift in attitude in a market sample. In the on-the-air market testing that followed, the revised commercial went through the roof. Calls came in as long as a month after the commercial had ceased to run. Some calls even came from markets where the commercial did not appear, indicating that the phone number had been written down and passed along!

Of course, we are talking about an agency and client with the will and the wherewithal to do special testing. But the method is available to all response advertisers. The principles are simple: ask your market questions, revise your work according to the answers you get, and keep refining until you are satisfied with the results.

Testing Physical Responses

A radically different approach to copy testing is the measurement of physiological responses to test commercials. The wave of the future in copy testing may deal extensively with the analysis of data obtained from monitoring brain waves, eye movements, voice pitch, and rate of perspiration. Agencies are exploring physical indicators because the testing of voluntary responses is inadequate. The established tests don't indicate with pinpoint accuracy what a person is responding to. Physiological methods claim greater specificity. By using devices such as lie detectors and electroencephalograms, researchers in involuntary behavior claim that they can isolate the moment arousal occurs and what causes it in a particular test commercial.

Physiological testing is usually more expensive per respondent than voluntary testing, and many research heads at leading agencies are skeptical of it. They claim that measures of autonomous nervous activity only indicate that a person is responding to a commerical in some way; they do not reveal whether a person likes or dislikes what he is responding to.

It is too soon to tell how useful physiological testing will be for advertising research. But because it measures involuntary physical responses, it is an intriguing subject for people who create response advertising. If a physiological pattern or curve leading to a direct response can be charted, it may be possible to determine what occurs when a viewer is moved to order something through a television commercial. If the contributing factors can be isolated, they can be duplicated in other commercials. This prospect is sufficiently promising to keep physiological testing in the direct response research picture for some time to come.

The RCA Music Service has already used physiological testing to measure the appeal of several of its support commercials. RCA chose the Consumer Behavior Center (CBC) in Richardson, Texas, to conduct the tests in which respondents were hooked up to a galvanic skin response device similar to the kind used in lie detectors. The apparatus measures the activation of sweat glands in the fingers and palms of the hand and is frequently used in measuring preview audience reactions to movies and record albums. CBC's findings in the RCA tests were presented in 1979 as a slide show at Direct Marketing Day in New York City. The testing revealed an impressive coincidence between test results and actual market performance.

Testing through Interactive Television

Considering that, in 20 years, interactive television may dominate the medium, the most meaningful method of testing available now may be the Warner/Amex QUBE System in Columbus, Ohio. QUBE is described at length later in this book but is mentioned here because it is the leading interactive system for testing commercials in the United States. QUBE subscribers take part in the tests in their own homes and can respond to the commercials immediately. While QUBE subscribers may not represent a target audience for many direct response products, Columbus, Ohio, is as close to cross-section of American life as you can get, and QUBE does provide a particularly fast and unique kind of testing in a natural environment.

Options for Testing

Let us assume at this point that you are ready to test. You have examined your competition, your market, and your product; you have positioned your product and have arrived at a marketing strategy. The question of the form in which you will present your test commercial to a sample of consumers remains.

You have a number of options. You can show your storyboard to people and ask questions about it. You can show the storyboard with a tape-recording of the voice-over. You can present a rough commercial for viewing. Or you can charge ahead, produce a finished commercial, and show that.

The finished commercial will be your most polished execution, and it will give you the best and most accurate measure of consumer response. But it may be too expensive to gamble this way. If you are committed to testing, it is beside the point to create a single finished version of an untested commercial.

Showing storyboards is also an inadequate method of testing. People react to a storyboard intellectually, not emotionally. Lacking sound and motion, the storyboard is a poor representation of a commercial; however, a storyboard test is probably better than no test at all.

A rough commercial is a necessary compromise between the expense of a finished commercial and the inadequacy of a storyboard. Many kinds of rough commercials are available, and many production companies create them at prices ranging from hundreds to thousands of dollars, depending on how elaborate you want the test commercial to be or how close it has to be to the real thing. You might even come away with a bargain, like the advertiser who made a rough commercial for several thousand dollars and liked it so much that he cancelled production of an expensive finished version and rolled out with his rough.

The simplest and least expensive rough involves a series of cuts and dissolves between storyboard frames plus a voice-over. The next step up is the animatic, which uses limited, Hanna-Barbera-type animation to simulate live action. Animatics are particularly good for direct response testing because direct response commercials involve a lot of demonstration and tend to go heavy on voice-overs. Naturally, an animatic leaves a lot to be desired if your creative approach hinges on the persuasiveness of on-camera talent.

Photomatics are test commercials that rely on photographs for an added degree of realism. They come with and without limited animation and have the obvious advantages of photography. Live-o-matics, or Videomatics, as described by its trademark holder, Windsor Total Video, is "limited animation on tape, using Chromakay and cells, manually moving pieces, stop motion working with art work and/or slides." This is the method to use if you want to see a real person talking on screen in any setting you choose, with anything happening that you choose. If you want to do a commercial in Tahiti with a cast of thousands, a Live-o-matic may be an important step to take before you get there.

Testing is a way to buy a little insurance that your commercial is going to perform at an acceptable level. But in a business where little guys as well as corporations have response commercials on television, it's difficult to establish minimum general guidelines and budgets for testing procedures. A certain marketing program may require elaborate testing in stages spread over a year. A small businessman may have only several thousand dollars to spend on a test and a few weeks to do it. But testing goes hand in hand with direct marketing. Direct response advertisers have conducted tests in their own ways for years, and this proclivity to test in mail and print can mean a lot to response television.

Split-Run Tests

John Caples, the dean of direct response copywriters who wrote the timeless "They laughed when I sat down at the piano . . . ," has made a strong case for testing television commercials through inexpensive direct response print advertising. In an article in the September 1977 issue of *Direct Marketing,* Caples suggests that a cheap, quick, and highly accurate method of testing a product's sales appeal is to use split-run copy testing of small print ads and base your TV commercial on the sales appeal of the ad that wins.

As an example of sales appeals to be tested, Caples uses *A,* low price, versus *B,* high quality. This is the "what you are saying" part of the commercial, not the "how you say it" part. Caples' way of testing in print applies to the noncreative aspects of price, offer, format, positioning, and marketing strategies.

In split-run testing, you can expose one half of a newspaper's circulation to quantity *A* and the other half to quantity *B*. Both exposures occur "on the same day, in the same newspaper, and in the same position in the newspaper." The cost of the test can be extremely modest, and, says Caples, *"This is the most accurate method of testing ever invented."*

Will a sales appeal that works in a newspaper be effective in other media? Caples says yes. "Of course it will. A good sales appeal is a good sales appeal no matter where you use it—in print media, in direct mail, in TV commercials."

The split-run method of copy testing calls for a classic A-B split in which the two different ads to be tested appear in alternate copies of a newspaper throughout its press run. A geographic split run with one ad running in the city edition and the second in the suburban papers is not adequate for a good test. More than two ads can be included in the split-run test, and space as small as two columns by seven inches can be used. The ads should have big bold headlines and should stress a particular sales appeal. Test ads should include some sort of direct response offer that will allow people to express their interest in what they have read. But, as Caples points out, it may be better to bury your offer to eliminate indiscriminate coupon clippers in order to get an exact measure of how many people were interested enough to read your ad through to the end.

Caples makes it clear that you use print to test *what* you are going to say on television, not *how* you are going to say it. Creative concepts for television commercials can be tested by using the methods previously described. There are times when it will seem that the most meaningful test of all is to run two commercials against each other on the air. And there are some people who like to go full speed ahead. Running two commercials is similar to split-run testing in print, but you cannot split a television market and expose every other viewer to a second commercial. So you do the next best thing—you run your two commercials in similar markets. Depending upon the product or the service you are offering, the difference between markets may be negligible.

In addition to testing different creative executions in similar markets, you may also use this method to test two-minute versus one-minute, or 30-second versus 60-second versions of a commercial. If the shorter commercial performs well, you'll save where it counts the most—in the cost of media. The only way to find out is to test.

Real World Testing

Now we are talking about testing in the real world. As much as today's copy-testing services try to replicate real life, there is no substitute for results from the field. The difference between a testing environment and real life is vast. Researchers try hard to compensate for this and do their best to supply what is missing in the research environment, but they can only do so much.

For one thing, any commercial that is on the air appears in a complex environment. It pops up bracketed between other commercials, during a particular program, on a particular channel, on a certain day. It appears in an individual's home where the furnace may have just broken. It appears on a particular day when the weather may drive people out of the house or keep them at home. Given all the variables that may influence behavior, it is clear that a single exposure to a commercial in either a testing situation or in real life is not enough to measure its effectiveness.

Response Television Testing

Multiple exposure to a commercial is particularly important in direct response. Whether we are talking about multiple exposure during a single program, a single evening, a single media effort of several weeks' duration, or continued exposure to the commercial through subsequent media efforts, multiple exposure to a direct response commercial has a direct bearing on sales.

When you plot the response rate for a successful direct response commercial, you will usually notice a build-up effect. A commercial has to run a number of times before people really start ordering. This is as true for the commercial running several times in one program as it is for the one running day after day for weeks. Although there are good days and bad days for response, as there are good and bad times of the day and good and bad seasons, media buyers hope that they will be able to run a commercial until it passes the break-even point and performs acceptably, after which time the commercial is monitored daily until it exhausts itself and ceases to work in its market. Once the commercial is pulled, it may very well run again in the same market in the future when the whole cycle will be repeated.

It would be hard to predict the performance curve of a

response commercial through existing pretesting methods with so much of a commercial's performance based on multiple exposure. Actually, running a direct response commercial with a limited media schedule for testing is an important part of research.

The media strategy for direct response commercials is based on testing in real life. If a commercial performs well in several test markets—usually anywhere from five to ten—more markets are bought and response rates are monitored. When the commercial wears itself out in a market, it is taken off the air and tried someplace else. All of this is real-life testing because media planners must continually monitor and evaluate results to expand their media base. Independent media services, some of whom charge their clients less than the standard agency commission, are available to anyone who wants to use television. Some will arrange for the production of direct response television commercials if required.

I mention this because there are still direct marketers who rule out television for themselves because they don't want to pay what they imagine will be an inordinately high agency fee. Many agencies cannot, in fact, afford to provide services for clients with modest budgets, but an independent media service can have your commercial on the air for surprisingly little money. Bear in mind, however, that amateurs fail repeatedly in response television. It is a remarkably wide-open field for any small businessman who can afford to be on television with a direct response or lead-gathering commercial. But he had better know what he is doing or at least know enough to pick a copy writer, producer, and media buyer who know what they are doing.

By the time your commercial has made it to the on-the-air testing phase, you will have made determinations about positioning, creative execution, your target audience, the time of day, and the part of the country you will run it. One way to see if you have made good choices is to come as close as you can to making a split-run print test using a single television market. John Caples recommends this for testing consumer commercials, but the method can be used for direct response commercials as well. The idea is to run alternate versions of a commercial at the same time of day in one market on alternate weekdays for two weeks. Commercial A runs Monday, commercial B runs Tuesday, and so on through Friday, beginning the second week with commercial B on Monday. At the end of the test, you will have exposed both commercials to close to the same market an equal number of times. By comparing responses to the two commercials, you can tell immediately which of the two came out ahead.

The more common way to test different executions is to run

the commercials at the same time of day in similar markets and compare results. Admittedly, this doesn't eliminate as many variables as the Caples consumer advertising method does, but depending on what you are offering, the variables might not make a difference. In a sense, using similar markets might give you a purer test because two executions of the same commercial running on alternate days in the same market might be reinforcing each other. The reinforcement would be a confusing variable which would not figure into the commercial's performance beyond the testing phase.

A commercial is tested on the air prior to roll out by running it in several markets where you have reason to believe it will do well because the markets have a proven number of viewers who shop by mail. The way your commercial performs in these markets will tell you if there are regional biases against your product or your method of selling it. It may tell you the best time of day to run your commercial or whether a movie works better for you than a soap opera. Since the object of direct marketing is to roll out as much as possible, affordable markets are usually chosen in different parts of the country to see if the commercial can make it on a nationwide basis. In total, there are well over 200 TV markets. Typical direct response markets that are used again and again to see how commercials perform include: Washington, D.C.; Chicago; Des Moines; Cedar Rapids; Los Angeles; St. Louis; Philadelphia; Portland; Seattle; Atlanta; New Orleans; Cleveland; Sacramento; Phoenix; Dallas/Fort Worth; and Houston.

Naturally, direct response markets are chosen with regard to what the commercial has to say. There is no general rule for picking markets and rolling out. The entire media schedule should be custom-tailored to the commercial by an expert. (For a discussion of time buying for direct response TV, see Appendix B.)

Standards for Testing and Scoring

You can talk about research and testing forever, but it doesn't mean a thing if the people who create response commercials don't pay more than lip service to research. Creative and research departments fought each other for a good many years in general advertising until the battle reached a point where creative people would grudgingly tolerate researchers and use their findings in creative executions.

But it should be different in direct marketing, a discipline with a long tradition of testing in mail and print. Creative people in direct response have been deeply involved in testing as a matter of course. So prejudices against research shouldn't be as harsh as they were when research was gaining a foothold elsewhere on Madison Avenue. Research is just another tool to be used creatively. In interpreting and applying knowledge gained through research, people working in response television will benefit most if they have a consistent attitude about what should be happening in a response commercial. One way to maintain that attitude is to have definite standards for creative work that can be used to score and rate response commercials.

Many agencies outside of direct response have developed their own scoring systems to rate commercials prior to production and to assist in the postmortem after their commercials are on the air. When used prior to the production of a commercial, a scoring system serves as a set of pretest guidelines. If the proposed commercial satisfies the scoring criteria, it is ready for testing and production. Any system of scoring creative work can be used, at best, almost imperceptibly or, at worst, heavy-handedly. Any scoring system that hampers creativity defeats its own purpose. The system should really be nothing more than a checklist of the important elements to include in a commercial to make it successful.

The standards for scoring commercials that come from general agencies are mostly designed to help a commercial break through the clutter of its television environment and stand out enough to communicate its information in a memorable way. Since general advertising isn't concerned with immediate feedback, its scoring criteria have limited application for our purposes. The criteria are more useful for scoring direct response support commercials that closely resemble traditional commercials. Nevertheless, scoring criteria from general advertising provide sensible guidelines for effective one-way communication through television, and they should be kept in mind when any commercial is written and tested.

Most traditional scoring systems ask that commercials be simple, believable, original, relevant to their target audiences, and empathetic. The systems rate commercials on their ability to attract attention immediately and hold viewers' attention. Their criteria were chosen to help produce commercials that stick in the mind and do special jobs, such as getting people to try a new product or change brands. The criteria are all relevant for direct response commercials, but some are more important than others. We'll examine each point in a little more detail and add several others of special importance for direct response.

Simplicity

The information in a commercial having to do with sales appeal, product, and offer should be as simple as possible, particularly in direct response commercials where legal mandates can be undesirably complex. Your creative approach may be complex. You may have a commercial that tells its story with sixty cuts, a dozen audio tracks, and a dozen supers, but the information being communicated should be simple, clear, and pointed. If a direct response commercial seems like it is going to be bogged down in details describing the product, the way it will be delivered, and instructions for ordering it, you would do well to keep things simple. Deal with these elements in a creative way, rather than having a "creative" portion of the commercial that is out of keeping with an informational portion. Real simplicity makes all of the elements in a commercial look like parts of the same thing. This simple unity helps viewers pay attention to your commercial because nothing jarring or disjointed is there to throw them a curve and shake their involvement. Remember that people think about all sorts of things while they are watching television, and those thoughts are probably far more interesting and absorbing than anything you have to say. So don't dilute the strength of your commercial with a message that is too complicated.

Believability

A commercial has to be believable, and making it believable is what separates good writers from hacks. It either has to be believable in itself or, to adopt Coleridge's rule for drama, it has to cause someone to suspend disbelief. Believability is particularly important in response advertising because so many people think that response commercials are intrinsically dishonest. Calling for immediate action as they do, direct response commercials have to seem more honest than other commercials, or they have to have a pitch that is engrossing enough to cause people to abandon their ordinary standards of judgment. No one will buy anything if they don't believe your commercial, and a sure way of failing to reach the non-response-buying consumer is to plod along using the tired old formulas of response television that have failed to ring true with the majority of American consumers.

Originality

Demand originality but suspect it. You'll have a breakthrough only with work that's original, but originality for its own sake is useless. Would-be poets, comics, and screenwriters who haven't learned that they are writing advertising copy can be original and fail miserably. Originality in creative work will get people to watch your commercial through to the end and more than once. It will help your commercial reach a wider audience. But unless it is the kind of originality that helps to produce a direct response, unless it can be tied to a mechanism that triggers ordering, it is wasted time and wasted thought.

Relevance and Empathy

Guidelines for relevance and empathy are met by confirming the viewer's experience. We want viewers to relate to what is being said and to project themselves into what's going on in the commercial. We often accomplish this through the personal, one-to-one tone of direct response advertising. If the commercial succeeds in making the viewer feel that he alone is being spoken to, these guidelines have probably been met. Commercials that are relevant and empathetic are believable, and they are believable because they are simple.

Attention

Advertising agencies have found that a commercial loses its audience if it doesn't grab their attention in the first few seconds. A commercial can satisfy all of the previous creative guidelines, but if it doesn't satisfy this one, the general advertiser must send his creative team back to the drawing board. The same applies even more to a direct response commercial, because most people turn off to direct response commercials in general. If we want those people, we've got to grab their attention; and because we want an order, we have to hold their attention from beginning to end. A direct response commercial that opens in a new and interesting way and follows through with originality could make customers out of people who might have otherwise dismissed the effort as "just another one of those junky call-in commercials."

The previous scoring criteria from general advertising are concerned mainly with recall and persuasion after exposure to commercials. Although they are useful in response television, we need specific standards for producing positive direct responses.

Motivation

The power to motivate viewers is the most important factor in a direct response commercial. We can call it the "Magic M." Does the commercial have a kind of *momentum* built into it that will carry a viewer to the point of making a direct response? Does it *motivate* the viewer to respond? In short, does it *move* the viewer along, or does it make him too much of a spectator? The words momentum and motivation have their roots in the Latin word *movere,* to move, which is literally what a direct response commercial must do. Every direct response commercial should include elements in its theme, tone, or structure that make a response the logical conclusion of having seen the commercial. The actual response might best be thought of as the completion of a circuit. When a viewer rises and dials the telephone, he or she is supplying the missing part of the circuit. The circuit is much more likely to be completed if the logical conclusion of the action of the commercial is a response. A commercial that has an invitation to respond simply tacked on to it should probably be thought through once again.

Understandability

When people shop by mail, they must understand all the details of their purchase. There can't be any loose ends in direct response commercials; therefore, explanations should be clear and complete, particularly those concerned with cash commitments. A question in the viewer's mind only stands in the way of action or leads to a misunderstanding that results in the consumer's dissatisfaction. A commercial that is clear answers all the questions it raises.

Security

The typical television customer wants to be reassured that it is safe to order. If a product or an advertiser is new and not nationally known, the viewer should be told that it is safe and why it is safe. Some guarantee of trial without risk, guaranteed satisfaction, or money back if requested should be included in response commercials because of the widespread and not unfounded fear of being ripped off.

Ease of Ordering

Don't diminish the comfort and convenience of shopping at home by making it difficult to order. A telephone number (sometimes an address) is the most important part of a direct response commercial, and it should come as no surprise to the viewer that he is going to be invited to call or write. Keep the number on the screen long enough to do the job; it shouldn't flash by the viewer in a blur. Once again, the minimum on-screen time for a telephone number is 15 seconds in a 60-second commercial and 20 seconds in a two-minute commercial, and it should be repeated out loud at least three times.

Given the demands of different creative strategies, positioning, offers, products, and pricing, it may not always be possible to follow every guideline for every commercial. But an attempt should be made to keep the guidelines in mind. In summary, they are:

1. Simplicity
2. Believability
3. Originality
4. Relevance and Empathy
5. Attention
6. Motivation
7. Understandability
8. Security
9. Ease of ordering

If we think in terms of a ten-point scale, a commercial meeting all of the criteria would score a perfect 10. But since some criteria are more important than others, we can simplify matters by recognizing value in each and applying those values proportionately to the needs of each commercial. A commercial selling a product that is being introduced for the first time may be light on originality but needs to be particularly believable. A commercial whose target audience is motivated to begin with— because the offer is in keeping with who they are and what they need—may downplay motivation and emphasize understandability. A perfect score of 10 will not guarantee a perfect commercial. But it is something to aim for, knowing that by achieving a perfect score, a conscientious effort was made to guarantee success.

Scoring, testing, and other research on response commercials is a formalized dialogue with the consumers. Beneath the formal aspect of that dialogue is raw communication—asking questions in a sufficiently open way so you can recognize the truth when it comes back to you. Beyond the importance of all research is the need for response television people to have an open and questioning attitude and be willing to meet their customers face to face. We'll either sharpen our sales instincts by watching people shop and by meeting them and asking them questions, or we will be unprepared to do our best in interactive telecommunications, which is where advertising is headed and which, in the final analysis, is based on the old one-on-one.

6
Television—
The Eye Has It

Of the many charges aimed at television, none is more damning than the accusation that it turns adults into children. As psychiatrist Eugene D. Glynn sees it:

> Television satisfies special needs centering around the wish for someone to care, to nurse, to give comfort and solace. These infantile longings (in adults) can be satisfied only symbolically, but how readily the television set fits in. Warmth, sound, constancy, availability, a steady giving without ever a demand for return, the encouragement to complete passive surrender and envelopment— all this and active fantasy besides. Watching these adults one is deeply impressed with their unconscious longing to be infants in mother's lap.*

Glynn is not entirely correct; television does not give steadily without ever demanding anything. Conventional broadcast television demands exposure to massive doses of advertising in return for "free" programming.

Nevertheless, the criticisms of the child-making aspects of television are not surprising when you consider television as a mass marketing tool. When you sell goods on a grand scale, it's easier if your market judges less, responds to simplistic statements and emotional appeals, and fails to distinguish between real and manufactured needs—in short, if the market is childlike.

---

*Eugene D. Glynn, "Television and the American Character—A Psychiatrist Looks at Television," in *Television's Impact on American Culture* (East Lansing, Michigan State University Press, 1956), William Elliott, ed.

The Ultimate Medium

Since its introduction to the public at the New York World's Fair of 1939, television has been praised as the ultimate communications, information, and entertainment medium—an industrial benefit of the highest order in the public interest. To the public, television was free entertainment. At the same time, spokesmen for the industry made it perfectly clear to businessmen that television was the chief means of their chief end. Almost as soon as television went commercial on July 1, 1941, the National Broadcasting Company, holder of the first United States commercial television license, had signed nearly a dozen advertising contracts.

Only a few thousand television receivers were in operation when television became an advertising medium. By the time it had become a mass medium less than a decade later, the domination of television by business, and therefore TV commercials, would raise questions about its misuse and its negative influence on viewers. *Direct marketers who want to encourage a shift in consumer behavior from traditional shopping patterns to buying through the box must consider the arguments against television and its advertising, because these surely play a part in consumer reluctance to make retail purchases directly through television.*

George Orwell conjured the most terrifying vision of television in *1984*. In the novel's world of Big Brother, television is used for surveillance and control. Television is interactive, beaming out propaganda and spying on its audience. To turn off a set and interrupt its surveillance is a crime. For Orwell, the invention that brought the world into the home overwhelms the home, erasing individualism and self-determination.

By juggling the title, *1984,* you come up with the novel's publication date, 1948. Orwell was not projecting into the future; he was expanding on the present at a time when the sale of TV sets was burgeoning in postwar America. Television became a mass medium in 1948. The number of stations on the air went from 17 to 41, the number of cities served rose from 8 to 23, and the sale of sets increased 500 percent over the previous year. The TV audience multiplied 4,000 percent compared to 1947. Orwell sensed what was happening and multiplied its implications, numerically and politically.

Today virtually every American watches television. There's a box in 98 percent of all homes, and nearly half of the homes have two or more sets. Young people who finish high school in 1984 will have spent at least 2,000 more hours watching television than they will have spent in the classroom. The average viewer watches more than seven hours of television a day, a figure that rises with growing unemployment as does demand for more video hardware and software. In addition to watching more standard TV fare than ever, more viewers are shelling out for bigger and brighter screens, for cable, pay TV, video cassette recorders, video games, and video disks. Entertainment boomed in the Depression of the thirties, and the harder life becomes the more people turn to television to fight off depression and exhaustion.

Anything looming as large as television did in 1948 was bound to disturb such socially conscious writers as George Orwell. However, television has continued to provoke writers' imaginations to the present day. More recently, television has been portrayed as an insidious tranquilizer used by totalitarian governments to keep citizens in line. François Truffaut's film of Ray Bradbury's *Farenheit 451* (the temperature at which books catch fire and burn) features interactive television as the principal leisure activity in a society where reading, and the individualism it encourages, is criminal. In the movie *THX 1138,* directed by George Lukas, the faceless proletariat confess their sins against the state to interactive TV monitors that dispense tranquilizers as penance.

Television is frightening because it is seductive, so seductive that it has grown to its present proportions. And beginning with the apple in the Garden of Eden, we have criticized that which attracts us. Despite criticism, apples and television remain popular. Several scholars, in fact, insist that large segments of the audience don't watch programs—they watch television.

Rolf B. Meyerson put it this way in his article "Social Research in Television," from *Mass Culture: The Popular Arts in America* (The Free Press of Glencoe, 1957, Bernard Rosenberg and David White, eds.):

> The entertainment that is TV is not simply an accretion of entertainment programs, it is the television set and the watching that entertains. Viewers seem to be entertained by the glow and the flow. . . . Television succeeds because it is there!!

This statement figures in many arguments against television. Television is insidious because it encourages passivity, and passive people are easily influenced and controlled. It is a case often raised by humanists and consumer advocates; however, businessmen, who have seen countless TV commercials fail, argue to the contrary. People are not readily influenced. Commercials succeed, and then only sometimes, when they reflect what the public already believes and transfer symbols of those beliefs to goods.

Television's Reassuring Stability

Controversy aside, television is the most stable American institution: it is a constant companion, it sticks to its schedule, and it beams out the message that America goes on. Except for the times it merges with reality—as in coverage of critical congressional hearings, the Chicago Democratic Convention of 1968, Viet Nam, the moon landing, John Kennedy's assassination, and Watergate—television glows along, unchallenging and innocuous, the most comforting and reassuring institution we have in these times of high anxiety.

Television commercials are even more consistent than the medium itself. If television is the most stable thing going, commercials are its underpinning. Commercials are absurdly optimistic in a pessimistic world. Every commercial says that what it's selling can make life better for the consumer. The face of American commercialism, called advertising, is always a pretty face that only smiles. No matter how cynical and beaten people become, they will always glance at another pretty face. It is the "all-is-well" reassurance of television that keeps people glued to the glow and the flow.

What will happen when watching TV requires more viewer participation, as direct marketing encourages? What will happen if television becomes widely interactive? Will *using* rather than just *watching* television make people more dependent on it? Hopefully not. Increased viewer participation implies more control over the medium by the viewer. Direct marketers who promote home shopping through television will find that they are also promoting increased consumer autonomy. Their difficult task is to determine the balance between the passive and active modes of behavior that leads to sales.

Television history offers one example after another of people's willingness to watch and participate. Since television caught fire in the late 1940s, many things other than direct response commercials have encouraged people to respond directly to television. Today's "Sesame Street" and "The Electric Company," which stress involvement to encourage learning, were preceded in the 1950s by the more frivolous but equally involving "Winky Dink." "Winky Dink" asked youngsters to stick a plastic sheet on their TV screens so they could draw at home what they saw on television. Naturally, the "Winky Dink" people marketed a play-along kit.

There is no reason, incidentally, why the "Winky Dink" approach couldn't be used in direct marketing promotions today. If you give the consumer enough time to trace a symbol from his TV screen onto a sheet of paper in return for some reward, you might just find that a large segment of viewers would take to the idea.

John Gnagy's popular "You Are an Artist" show in the 1950s invited viewers to draw pictures step by step with the television artist. The show ran for years and, as with "Winky Dink," you needed a special kit to really participate.

Equally inviting are telethons that encourage viewers to call in pledges of money for various worthy causes. So are game shows that ask viewers to play along at home and, sometimes, compete for prizes.

TV evangelist Oral Roberts is an absolute genius when it comes to getting viewers to participate in the action on their screens. In the 1950s, Roberts invariably wound up his weekly revival show with a prayer for the afflicted. Raising his hand to the TV camera, Roberts would call upon the viewers at home to get out of their chairs, walk over to the TV set, kneel down, and place their hands over his on the TV screen. There's no doubt that thousands did what they were asked, which is noteworthy for direct marketers. If the history of direct response television advertising is indicative of anything, it demonstrates that what works under the tent for God can work on the tube for Mammon.

Viewer Behavior: Clues for Direct Marketers

How to make things work is another question. More than ever, direct marketers are trying to discover what works on television and how viewers behave.

We know that the season, the time of day, and the type of programming influence who watches television and how viewers react to commercials. The television year is divided into quarters: January–March, April–June, July–September, October–December. The first quarter is best for direct response advertisers because the cost of TV time is lower and most people watch television in the winter. Costs are also down in July, August, and September, but fair weather, longer daylight hours, and vacations reduce the audience significantly.

A television day is divided into four dayparts: daytime (sign-on to 4:00 P.M.), early fringe (4:00 P.M.to 8:00 P.M.), prime time (8:00 P.M. to 11:00 P.M.), and late fringe (11:00 P.M. to sign-off). Most people watch during prime time, with viewing of late fringe, early fringe, and daytime following in that order.

The phenomenon called "tuning inertia," which describes watching television in general rather than a specific program, keeps some people glued to the first channel they turn on. But commercials are responsible for a drop in viewer attention. The culprit often blamed is "clutter," the proliferation of 30-second announcements that makes people feel assailed by commercials. (The relatively long two-minute direct response spot may actually serve as an oasis within the clutter.)

Direct marketers often assume that the more attentive people are to the programs they watch, the less attentive they will be to direct response commercials. They also assume that viewers who watch programs in which they are not particularly interested, such as reruns of old movies, are more receptive to direct response messages because they aren't afraid to miss some of the program if they get up to call in an order. The opposite assumption is held in general advertising. Generalists say that people who are interested in programs they watch have better recall of the commercials that those programs carry. Although this is not a contradiction of the direct response experience, it challenges direct marketers to make viewer attention work for rather than against them. Attention could help to make sales if a means could be found to convert attention into interaction with television. What's more, the seeming inattention to reruns and old movies may actually be a more profound viewer attention— the familiar rerun serving as an automatic pilot, linking the viewer to the flow of the glow.

It's no surprise to say that television is addictive. What comes as a shock is the possibility that about half of the audience that's hooked on the tube suffers from darker addictions as well. A January 27, 1981, *New York Times* article by Dava Sobel reported that 49 percent of 420 QUBE viewers in Columbus, Ohio, admitted to being addicts or to having an addict in the family. Addiction was defined as "any obsessive or compulsive use of a substance to cope with pain of any kind and to produce a high." Overwork, overeating, and compulsive gambling were included in the definition. If the Columbus sample is representative of the country, direct marketers should at least be aware of the pathology of addiction in order to reach more viewers and reach them effectively.

Direct marketing has always stressed the need for an accurate audience profile. In-depth knowledge of this sort, particularly detailed psychographic data, is hard to come by for television. We know that television commercials have influenced behavior massively and dramatically *in some cases,* but we are generally at a loss to determine precisely *how* consumers react to television advertising. Research into this question is becoming more sophisticated but is proceeding slowly. Studies by social scientists and psychologists into consumer attitudes toward television commercials are surprisingly few. Not surprisingly, similar studies by businesses are well-kept secrets. But the need to know grows stronger as TV's direct marketing potential grows larger.

What we know about viewers' attitudes toward television and TV commercials comes largely from two major studies commissioned by business. The first is the Roper Organization's 20-year review of public perceptions of television and other mass media between 1959 and 1978.

Sponsored by the Television Information Office, the Roper Report reveals that television became the dominant mass medium in 1963 and that, with the advent of the 1980s, it continues to be the most believable medium. To the public it is the first and most credible source of news, the preeminent source of information. Television presently enjoys a two-to-one advantage over newspapers as a news source, and this tendency is expected to increase with the increased movement of the urban middle class to the suburbs, where city papers will be unable to supply suburban information needs.

So television is important. It is believed. The report concludes with some interesting findings: "1. The American public continues to endorse the commercially sponsored system of broadcasting. 2. While criticism exists, critics are in the minority. 3. Most people agree that having commercials is a fair price to pay for getting their programs. . . ."

Then why is it so hard to make commercials work? If television is so important to people and if they endorse commercial broadcasting, why do commercials turn people off? The Roper Report offers two important clues.

Of those who felt that having commercials on television is *not* a fair price to pay for being able to watch television, the majority believe that: "1. Commercials are more objectionable than programming. 2. Criticism of commercials is fairly evenly divided between the number of commercials that are on, their content, and the interruptions they cause in the programs."

To get a better fix on the public's case against television advertising, it is helpful to look at a second study: the American Association of Advertising Agencies (AAAA) study titled *Con-*

sumer Judgment in Advertising, planned and supervised by academicians from Harvard and the Massachusetts Institute of Technology in cooperation with the Opinion Research Corporation. Published in 1968, it remains the most comprehensive research project ever undertaken in public attitudes toward advertising. The Roper Report of a decade later would confirm its finding that the public supports the broad, economic role of advertising in national life. The AAAA study also shows that people have serious doubts about the truth of advertising and react adversely to advertising when it offends taste and insults intelligence.

There are serious implications here for direct marketers, especially as response advertising on television is getting a new look. Paying attention to how consumers view television advertising can help us arrive at that new look. Once again in our ground breaking, we will have to rely on information from general advertising. There is very little information about the behavior of in-home shoppers to guide us. Psychographic data about direct response television shoppers are virtually nonexistent. A lot of vague theorizing on how people feel about direct response advertising has been offered on the basis of insufficient data and inaccurate measurement. But we really don't know how people respond to response outside of the gross data provided by sales figures, which are mostly unobtainable.

The AAAA study comes to three conclusions that can have bearing on direct response television advertising to come.

1. People pay conscious attention to relatively few advertisements of the many to which they are potentially exposed daily.
2. When an advertisement *does* engage the consumer's attention, it is very likely not to strike him as *annoying* or *offensive,* but it is not very likely to strike him as *enjoyable* or *informative,* either.
3. Advertisements which offend some may annoy others, but these same advertisements may also inform some and even entertain others. [There is] no unanimity among consumers about individual advertisements: one consumer's annoyance is another's entertainment, another's information, another's offense. Many consumers pay no attention to these same advertisements.

At first glance, this is chaos to an advertiser who is looking for guidance. People don't pay much attention to advertising; most advertising doesn't move people one way or another. Reactions to advertising are entirely subjective. Yet beneath the chaos there are principles for order and direction.

Consumer Values and Successful Advertising

That people pay little attention to advertising leaves no doubt that a response commercial must attract attention fast and hold it as long as the commercial lasts. It's easy to attract attention. The problem is how to maintain attention so the viewer's reaction is favorable and not neutral or annoyed. *Consumer Judgment of Advertising* tells us that people dislike advertising when they suspect that it is false and misleading or interruptive and repetitive. Advertising is perceived as false when it fails to confirm viewers' experience or contradicts their values. People are neutral about advertising when they are disinterested in the product advertised or find the commercial typical. Either way, a neutral or hostile reaction means no sale. But we stand a better chance of making sales if we rely on those elements the AAAA study tells us consumers find enjoyable in advertising: *information, self-reference,* and *entertainment.*

Consumers value information in commercials above everything else. They consider advertising informative when they learn something about a product, its function, or its price. Consumers also equate personal involvement and truth with information.

Information linked to persuasion is the heart of direct response advertising. Since the goal of direct response advertising is a direct sale, it always has a lot of explaining to do and tends to be information-heavy. Response advertising's need to inform, coupled with the consumer's predisposition to favor informative advertising, gives response a distinct edge over mere image-making and puffery. But the advantage is often missed. The information any given commercial has to get across is sometimes seen as a stumbling block, a nuisance to get through as quickly as possible to satisfy legal requirements.

When information is sandwiched in and rattled off between the "creative" portions of a commercial, an opportunity to persuade is overlooked. What a customer is being asked to pay, what he gets for his money, and how and when he is going to get it is information that can be expressed persuasively rather than boringly. Moreover it is information that touches consumers personally, thus creating the "involvement" that they have indicated is important to them. Facts should be dramatized with an eye to creating empathy and involvement. As a creative resource, product specifications and the terms of an offer can be a gold mine.

Many consumers felt that advertising was informative when they could identify with it. When consumers feel that the actors in commercials are like themselves and have the same needs, desires, and problems, they react favorably and feel informed. Empathy occurs when advertising reflects the viewer's personal experience, but when it contradicts personal experience the viewer is likely to find it both annoying and offensive. The contradiction of personal experience turns off more viewers than any other single factor, more than repetition, absurdity, or abrasive creative treatments.

The moral is clear. If information and confirmed personal experience create favorable impressions, the direct response copywriter must *inform relevantly*. The consumer relies on his own experiences to judge whether a commercial is true or false. In getting to the truth about a product, a writer must also use his own experiences. Response commercials need a new realism of facts enlivened by the truth of personal experience. This new realism won't look like the neorealism that revolutionized film-making after World War II, but it might have a similar impact.

We have been talking about not offending viewers so we may stand a better chance of getting people to respond to a commercial. Commercials that make no impression on consumers add up to as many lost customers as commercials that offend. In the AAAA survey, the reason given most often as to why advertising made no impression one way or the other was that there was a *sameness* about the advertising treatment. This should be a clear warning to direct marketers who believe in formula and imitation. But record collections, exercise devices, magazines, kitchen gadgets, and continuity programs continue to be sold in the same old way. Here the facts contradict practice, and the facts call for innovation and imagination.

We can use information to the utmost, and we can produce commercials with which people empathize. But even if we do these things, the TV watcher might tune us out mentally—unless our commercials are enjoyable. And what makes a commercial enjoyable is its creative treatment.

Subjectivity in Direct Response

Consumers cite humor, music, talented actors, and just plain good looks in a production as things that make commercials enjoyable. Yet in advertising as in everything else, one man's meat is another man's poison. What's funny to me isn't necessarily funny to you. We can only assume, then, that any creative approach must be distinctive to avoid making a neutral impression. Advertising is on the right track when it is vivid and emphatic. Since every judgment made about it is going to be subjective, there is no right or wrong—only impressive or unimpressive.

Subjectivity governs the perception of advertising. One doesn't have to be in the business long to discover that it governs the creation of advertising as well. Recognizing the importance of subjectivity in advertising from start to finish will make it easier for direct marketers to test creative treatments, not because those treatments satisfy one's personal taste but because they are emphatic and original. From the 1970s through the present day, the major trend in fine arts in this country has been random individual expression. Movements have come and gone quickly, but no single dominant idea (such as social realism in the 1930s) has governed expression or the perception of it as movements have in the past. Likewise, random individual expression in advertising is perfectly in keeping with the times. We've all spotted the chaos beneath the surface of order in America and, for the moment, there is no clear direction for this country, its art, or its advertising. There won't be a direction until a major social or economic change alters American values and sets the course advertising will have to follow. Rosser Reeve's hard sell is not definitive, nor is the flair of Jerry Della Femina, nor is the bold and tasteful wit of William Bernbach. There are many ways to do a commercial, but the way that fulfills the most direct marketing principles *and* makes the strongest impression is the approach worth testing. The need for original creative treatments to offset the sameness in advertising reemphasizes the need to upgrade the creative part of many direct marketing operations today.

Ethical Guidelines for Direct Marketers

The biggest stumbling block to popular acceptance of response television advertising probably isn't the consumer reaction to particular commercials but their negative reaction to response advertising per se. People will remain skeptical until direct marketers take the necessary steps to lift the suspicion that clouds their industry.

The Direct Mail/Marketing Association took one step in the right direction when it issued a series of ethical guidelines for direct marketing business practices and broadcast advertising.

Among 28 guidelines suggested for ethical business practice, 15 have particular relevance for television advertisers.

1. Direct response marketers should make their offers clear and honest. They should not misrepresent a product, service, publication, or program and should not use misleading, partially true, or exaggerated statements. All descriptions and promises should be in accordance with actual conditions, situations, and circumstances existing at the time a promotion is made. Direct response marketers should operate in accordance with the Better Business Bureau's (BBB) Basic Principles contained in the BBB Code of Advertising and be cognizant of and adhere to the postal laws and regulations, and other laws governing advertising and transaction of business by mail, telephone, and the print and broadcast media.

2. Direct response marketers should not disparage any person or group on grounds of sex, race, color, creed, age, or nationality.

3. Solicitations, regardless of medium used, should not contain vulgar, immoral, profane, or offensive matter nor promote the sale of pornographic material or other matter not acceptable for advertising on moral grounds.

4. Photographs and artwork representing or implying representation of a product or service or fund-raising program for nonprofit organizations should be faithful reproductions of the product, service, or aid offered by the fund-raising program. All should be current and truly representative. All descriptions and promises should be in accordance with actual conditions, situations, and circumstances existing at the time of the promotion. Photographs and artwork representing or implying situations related to a product, service, or program should be in accordance with the facts. If models are used, clear disclosure of that fact should be made in immediate conjunction with the portrayal.

5. If laboratory test data are used in advertising, they should be competent as to source and methodology. Reference to laboratory test data should not be used in support of claims which distort or fail to disclose the true test results.

6. Direct response marketers should not use unsupported or inaccurate statistical data or testimonials originally given for products or services other than those offered, or testimonials making statements or conclusions known to be incorrect. If testimonials are used, they should contain no misstatement of facts or misleading implications and should reflect the current opinion of the author.

7. Direct response marketers should not make exaggerated price comparisons, exaggerated claims on discounts or savings, or employ fictitious prices.
8. Direct response marketers should sufficiently identify themselves in every solicitation to enable the consumer to contact them.
9. Direct response marketers should be prepared to make prompt delivery of orders. Any delay should be promptly reported to the customer informing him of his right to consent to the delay or obtain a refund.
10. The terms and conditions of guarantee should be clearly and specifically set forth in immediate conjunction with the guarantee offer. Performance guarantees should be limited to the reasonable capabilities and qualities of the product or service advertised.
11. When products or services are offered on a satisfaction-guaranteed or money-back basis, any refunds requested should be made promptly. In an unqualified offer of refund or replacement, the customer's preference shall prevail.
12. Direct response marketers should not make offers which purport to require a person to return a notice that he does not wish to receive further merchandise in order to avoid liability for purchase price, unless all the conditions are first made clear in an initial offer that is accepted by the purchaser by means of a bona fide order. (For detailed specifications regarding Negative Option Plans, see Federal Trade Commission regulations.)
13. Unordered merchandise should not be sent unless such merchandise is clearly and conspicuously represented to be "free" and the recipient clearly informed of his unqualified right to treat it as a gift and to do with it as he sees fit, at no cost or obligation to him.
14. A product or service which is offered without cost or obligation to the recipient may be unqualifiedly described as "free." "Free" may also be used conditionally where the offer requires the recipient to purchase some other product or service, provided all terms and conditions are accurately and conspicuously disclosed in immediate conjunction with the use of the term "free" and the product or service required to be purchased is not increased in price or decreased in quality or quantity.
15. Direct response marketers who sell instruction, catalogs, or merchandise-for-resale or who sell or rent lists should not use misleading or deceptive statements with respect to the earning possibilities, lack of risk, or ease of operation.

In its broadcast advertising guidelines, the DM/MA notes that the principal types of direct response complaints involve misrepresentation and nondelivery of merchandise. Attempting to reduce these complaints and "promote more credibility in the eyes of the consumer and, thereby, more business for radio and television stations and their advertisers," the DM/MA advises that all commercials comply to the National Association of Broadcasters code. Getting NAB approval is a useful step toward fair and honest advertising insofar as the code is based on a number of existing legal requirements and FCC regulations. The code's proscriptions have to do mainly with maintaining standards for units of commercial time, upholding accepted social values, and weeding out unacceptable types of commercials—all of which is in the best interest of direct response advertising. The NAB code authority reviews thousands of commercials every year and provides some help in eliminating fraudulent, deceptive, and offensive broadcast advertising.

The DM/MA has some further suggestions to help broadcasters determine what is or is not acceptable advertising. Most of these guidelines can serve the people who create commercials as well.

1. Insure that the advertising message is presented with courtesy and good taste. Disturbing or annoying material should be avoided. Do not be afraid to ask for a revision in the commercial or a copy change if you feel the commercial has gone too far.
2. Experience trains your intuition. If an intuitive reaction tells you to check out an offer very throroughly, do so. Do not let it slip by.
3. If the business was "too easy to get" or if a large time buy came in "over the transom"—be suspicious.
4. Examine whether the commercial offers misleading descriptions or visual misrepresentations of any premiums or merchandise or gifts which would distort or enlarge their value in the minds of consumers.
5. If the offer is vague, do not approve it. If you have to read the copy through twice and you still do not know what you are getting, ask the advertiser for a clarification of the copy. Do not accept an offer unless it is clearly spelled out.
6. Insure that on-screen copy and/or the voice-over adequately specify the terms of the offer and the merchandise. Insure that on-screen crawls are readable. Be certain that they move slowly enough to be read by the average viewer. If the

consumer obtains unsatisfactory treatment from the advertiser, he will blame you (the broadcaster). Insure that both visual and audio claims support each other.
7. Make yourself the surrogate viewer or listener. Are the copy and/or pictures outlandish? Are the claims so strong as to be unbelievable?

Unfortunately, good intentions can't eliminate abuses. The NAB, DM/MA, and Better Business Bureau are voluntary organizations. Their self-regulation is voluntary. Although the NAB television code was adopted in 1952, it had little effect until a decade later when an authority was established to oversee its implementation. As late as 1976, stations could join NAB without subscribing to its code. DM/MA's Ethics Committee is in a similar position. The firmest measure it can take is to refer complaints to appropriate government or regulatory agencies. There is a clear need to establish the kind of authority to implement DM/MA guidelines that the NAB set up at the opening of the 1960s.

The DM/MA would do well to step up the regulation of direct response advertising, starting with television because broadcast is still the least-used response medium, and its regulation would be easier to administer than that of print and mail.

A direct marketing code authority for ethical television advertising could be authorized to award a seal of approval for commercials meeting its guidelines. It would be hoped that the appearance of the seal in code-approved commercials would have the effect that the Underwriters' Laboratory and Good Housekeeping seals have had in advertising—it would alert consumers that the product advertised had been examined with their best interests in mind. It would only take a second for the seal to appear at the start of a commercial in much the same way that a rating code message precedes a movie or a movie preview. It could also be included with the end tag. Consumer awareness of the difference between code-approved and unapproved commercials would encourage advertisers to seek regulation and would help to keep unethical advertisers off the air.

The effectiveness of self-regulation of this kind hangs on complex legal questions, and only a few points have been sketched here to promote further discussion. Ultimately, trade associations are unable to enforce compliance with their regulations because antitrust laws rule out the power of trade associations to control their memberships. Still, the NAB has made strides in consumer protection. The DM/MA could do likewise.

New Audiences for Direct Response

Widespread negative perception of response advertising on television has left direct marketers with only a small segment of television's vast audience. Excluding support advertising, which may appear on prime-time network television, direct response advertising is carried almost entirely by local stations and cable channels. This amounts to communicating with only a fraction of the total TV audience. During prime time we don't even have a slice of the pie; we're left with the crumbs as far as effective penetration of total TV homes is concerned.

Direct marketers have found it economically and strategically advantageous to use national-spot advertising on independent stations instead of buying time on national and broadly regional network programming. National-spot advertising is affordable. It literally lets TV direct marketers plot their campaigns on a map by offering a wide range of markets to test. An agency commission on time buys—national spot and otherwise—is usually 15 or 17.6 percent.

As advantageous as national-spot buying can be, however, prime-time network audiences still amount to the largest and most representative share of the market—a share direct marketers cannot afford to reach. Cut off from the networks by the cost of the time, direct marketers will find it useful to explore other television options in order to reach more viewers at a price they can afford. The most meaningful option is cable television. Cable's growth, if it is exploited, may spell a parallel growth for direct response advertising on television. The interactive future, which to a large extent *is* the future of direct marketing, depends on cable alone.

The increasing importance of Community Antenna Television (CATV) depends upon people's willingness to pay for additional benefits and services on the TV sets they own. Since cable's commercial introduction in 1950, more and more people have been willing to buy what cable sells: first, better reception and the reception of all three networks in inadequately serviced markets; and second, more programming and additional video options in all markets. It remains to be seen how many people will pay for additional cable services and what those services will be. But if the demand continues to grow, it will lead to a communications and advertising upheaval.

The networks are still the unchallenged leaders in the expanding television market. But cable operators are moving fast and may jolt network supremacy. Among the new forms of telecommunications distribution, the following are meaningful for direct marketers.

Basic Cable uses coaxial terrestrial cable to deliver off-the-air TV broadcast signals to subscribers who pay installation and monthly subscription fees. Over 4,000 systems are in operation and service every state. The average system offers about a dozen channels but could offer many more; for instance, Warner/Amex is contemplating a 125-channel system for New York City. Cable has grown by 500 percent in the last decade and numbers over 16,000,000 subscribers.

Pay-TV (or FeeVee) uses two basic transmission systems. Cable is used by such subscription services as Home Box Office (HBO) and Showtime, which present uncut movies, sports, and entertainment that are unavailable on standard television. Over-the-air subscription television, with half a dozen stations currently in operation, transmits a scrambled UHF signal that is decoded by a device hooked up to the subscriber's television set. There are no commercials on pay-TV at the present time, although this may change. In 1980 there were approximately 6,000,000 pay-TV subscribers.

Satellites beam broadcast signals back to earth without terrestrial wiring. They are used to transmit superstation and pay-TV signals to parabolic antennas (earth stations) which receive the signals for cable systems. Eight satellites are in operation: Western Union's Westar I, II, and III; RCA Americom's Satcom I and II; and COMSAT General's Comstar I, II, and III. A joint venture between COMSAT and Sears to provide satellite-to-home programming has been proposed.

Superstations are TV broadcast stations that have their signals "bounced" by satellite to distant cable TV systems. Ted Turner's WTBS-TV in Atlanta, Georgia, was the first superstation. It presently reaches over 6,000,000 cable subscribers, including viewers in Alaska, Hawaii, Puerto Rico, and the Virgin Islands. Other superstations are WGN-TV, Chicago; WOR-TV, New York City; and KTVU, Oakland-San Francisco. Because they sell broadcasters' programming (and commercials) to cable operators, the superstations have been accused of piracy. The controversy is likely to stay hot for some time to come.

In the third edition of his basic textbook, *Broadcasting in America,* Sidney Head observes that

> Cable systems . . . draw off advertising revenue that would otherwise support broadcasting. So far the cable market remains small. . . . But local cable systems united

into national cable networks by means of satellite relay interconnection could seriously undermine broadcasting's earning power as an advertising medium.

A national cable network would jeopardize broadcasting's ad revenues because cable would then be able to provide markets at a much lower cost per thousand. The lower rates would make it possible for more direct marketers to use more television than ever. With this prospect ahead, direct marketers would clearly benefit from working with cable early on, associating themselves closely with the medium, growing with it, even preempting it for direct marketing as much as possible. The time for national direct marketers to start with cable is now when a relatively small number of cable systems can accommodate commercials rather than a decade from now when many more systems will carry commercials and the use of the medium will be confusing to the uninitiated.

In 1978, Young & Rubicam's vice-president, William J. Donelley, placed cable penetrations into United States homes at 16.9 percent. The study which cited that figure went on to predict, somewhat optimistically, that the penetration would rise to 33 percent of United States households by Christmas Day 1981. That is important, Donelley said, because "we believe 30 percent penetration is the critical mass required of an electronic communications medium to become a broadbased advertising medium."

Cable operators argue that their currently smaller, specialized audiences are worth cultivating, pointing out that the demographics involved are a cut above those of traditional "lowest common denominator" broadcast audiences. Cable markets cost less, too. And there is no FCC regulation over cable program content or the length of commercials on cable television. (For a discussion of cable advertising costs and testing, see Appendix C.)

Cable services that don't now take advertising may do so in the future. A recent A.C. Nielsen report shows that pay cable services, such as HBO and Showtime, which do not accept advertising, are competing effectively with network programming. Many media observers believe that the pay services will eventually bracket their programs between blocks of messages.

The biggest commercial success in cable to date has been Ted Turner's Atlanta superstation. For the majority of direct marketers, WTSB is *the* TV goldmine. Turner also has a 24-hour cable news network which allows participating cable systems two minutes of local advertising per hour, with ten minutes set aside for national advertising.

Cable sportscasts by the Entertainment and Sports Programming Network of Bristol, Connecticut, have attracted more advertisers than Turner's newscasts. Initial advertisers included Anheuser-Busch, the *Wall Street Journal,* Pontiac, Hilton Hotels, the Air Force Reserve, Magnavox, Hertz, Showtime, Noxema, and Getty Oil, the network's owner. A second sports network, U-A Columbia Cablevision of Oakland, New Jersey, which markets the Madison Square Garden Network, entered into a trial arrangement with major legue baseball to cablecast 33 games in 1979. National advertisers such as Pabst, Tylenol, Uniroyal, and Gillette were on for 11 minutes per game at a cost of $650 per minute. Local systems received nine minutes for advertising.

The Satellite Program Network (SPN) division of Satellite Syndicated Systems cablecasts everything *but* sports just about 24 hours a day. SPN is set up to be totally advertiser-sponsored with about eight national and two local ad minutes per hour.

Other commercial cable systems include the Beverly Hills based Cinemerica Satellite Network, which is targeted at people over 50. It has five minutes of national advertising per hour and one minute for local systems. Washington, D.C.'s Black Entertainment Television claims to reach up to 5,000,000 households and offers 16 commercial minutes per two-hour programming segment. Another cable system is "The Women's Channel," the first network targeted completely toward adult women. It is produced by Satellite Syndicated Systems and features four new half-hour segments each weekday. Two minutes of local availability every half-hour are included in this advertising-supported network.

The Cable TV catalog, Cable Ad, is an interesting new cable marketing system. Airing about two hours a day, Cable Ad consists of segments showcasing products from participating catalog houses. Its direct marketing potential is obvious as is that of Washburn Associates' "Home Shopping Show" discussed previously.

The January 1980 issue of *Marketing Communications* reported on a month-long test of a half-hour Cable Ad program featuring 23 items from the catalog showroom chain, W. Bell and Company. As the magazine describes it: "Models were shown wearing items such as jewelry. Other items were photographed from transparencies. A two-minute product demonstration was given for Texas Instrument's Speak and Spell game."

The test was undertaken "to determine the best times of day for presenting various products," said Cable Ad's chairman of the board, Robert D. Burgener. Burgener also discovered that "there were strong correlations between people who had the print catalog in hand, and who were asked to order from the screen. People who didn't have the catalog wouldn't order. . . . The only way catalog marketing on TV will work is through strong print support."

This may or may not be true. The verdict on how people will react to product programming won't be in until this new marketing approach is given a full creative treatment. When as much thought goes into the creative approach and production values of a product program as goes into the marketing strategy, we will have a clearer picture of how people react to product shows; but we won't have it until then.

Burgener does not call "product programming" advertising. Cable operators shy away from the term, he says, because they think their customers will reject it. But Burgener feels that cable viewers will go for product programming because "It is advertising as advertising was originally meant to be. With the energy crisis let's try to think of TV a little differently. It has always been an entertainment medium. Now we're taking a channel available and also making it an informational service."

There's that word again, "information," the element consumers like best about advertising. We'll be hearing "information" used in place of "advertising" more frequently as cable audiences grow in number. Advertising on cable is likely to remain in the background for a time because it goes against the grain of the original concept of commercial-free cable and because cable has the potential to carry so much advertising. But whether you use "information," "product programming," or any other euphemism, the display of wares is advertising, as sure as corporate-funding announcements in cultural programs on educational television is public relations.

Mail-order catalogs, direct mail, and response print are the antecedents for this new school of television advertising that stresses information. Today's traditional TV commercials, like the beautifully photographed and edited mini-movies for Coke and Pepsi, will seem quaint and naïve compared to the newly emerging informative format for cable. The future on cable advertising won't mean who can paint the prettiest picture that will stick in your mind, but who can convey information most persuasively without seeming pushy.

Inconclusive or poor results from testing in-home shopping commercials on cable indicate that the road ahead is full of pitfalls. It may be that people are simply unfamiliar with cable as a direct shopping medium and will have to live with the idea for a while. As it now stands, cable audience data and ways to measure the viewing habits of cable subscribers are sadly lacking. But the promise of cable cannot be disregarded nor can plans to explore it be deferred by direct marketers. The opportunity for an advertiser to grow with a mass communications medium is too compelling to overlook, considering the way advertisers tend to influence and sometimes dominate their media. Commercial cable television, like direct marketing itself, was long overlooked as a medium to be reckoned with. Now it looks like the convergence of this maverick medium with our maverick method of marketing might turn into a partnership that would net the lion's share of consumer dollars nationwide and worldwide.

The first steps can be easy. As Robert Burgener describes it in a bulletin headed *Energy Savings Now:*

> Using some technology we are already familiar with, namely our telephones, and a shopping device we are all familiar with, the mail order catalog, many things can begin to happen right now. When we add the dimension of television to the print catalog, the still photos of products become animated and shoppers can see several views while an announcer's voice adds additional descriptive commentary. Products can be demonstrated and put through their paces in the same way one would find them presented by a salesperson in the store—but you didn't have to drive to the store for the show.
>
> For the consumer, shopping with what we call the *Cable Catalog* can mean saving trips to the store without sacrificing the right to visually sample as many items of interest as possible, in sufficient detail so as to make a well-informed choice. For the merchant this medium provides enough time and dimension to present products in a manner which is most likely to compete successfully for the consumer's attention.
>
> Cable television can provide this service on a separate *Shopper's Channel* without interfering with the commercial-free nature of its entertainment services. The Cable Catalog segments can be repeated several times of the day or week to develop the maximum cumulative reach, and the schedule of their specific showing times listed by advertiser and category can be mailed directly to the cable television subscriber.

Although cable advertising revenues have been unimpressive, satellite-cable telecommunications is the wave of the future and will be vital to advertising. As Americans become poorer, they'll need more inexpensive information, and seek more relief through entertainment. Television will meet both needs. By 1984, people will need more television than ever. And cable is more.

7
The Interactive Future

New video options will transform not only the face of broadcasting, but the lives of Americans as profoundly as the Industrial Revolution of the nineteenth century.
—Representative Lionel Van Deerlin, Chairman of the House Subcommittee on Communications, *Newsweek,* July 13, 1978

Historical distinctions between electronic media like the telephone and television . . . are breaking down and fading away. Traditional concepts are being blitzed by a revolution in the technology by which we communicate.
—Charles Ferris, Chairman of the Federal Communications Commission, *Panorama,* March 1980

Change can be perplexing, even frightening, when it doesn't head in a simple positive direction and when it has many causes that are hard to pin down. The coming of widespread interactive television would be one such life-altering change, and there is ample reason to be confused about it. What will happen and how it will happen hinge on nothing less predictable than the average person's willingness to pay for interactive systems and services, depending upon his real or imagined needs.

Interactive television will literally put the world at the fingertips of the consumer who can use his television to send and receive information to and from distant computers. But gaining the world can also mean losing something. Interactive television stands to eliminate retailing as we know it. We'll have to say good-bye not only to mom and pop at the corner store, but also to the clerks at the shopping mall and the supermarket. Malls and supermarkets have no real place in the interactive future because most retailing will be direct marketing.

Life will be "easier" when we can order merchandise directly through television. But it will also be harder if a struggle develops between those who can pay for interactive systems and those who cannot. Interactive antitheft services will, to some extent, protect goods obtained through interactive television against intruders who cannot afford those goods or their interactive means of access.

Two-way television will save us time and add to our leisure time. But who is to say that it will not remove us further than we already are from the world outside the home, substituting the TV screen for a world that developed variously in the first place because it was *not* instantly accessible.

Savings and Interactive Television

Saving energy and especially saving time are the strongest arguments that might sell consumers on the idea of two-way television. (In this country, where interactive development is strictly a business venture unlike government-sponsored developments abroad, the corporations working on American systems want to be sure that there's a market out there before they leap.) Saving time is particularly interesting for marketers because the way consumers feel about their time determines what they buy and how they buy it. Currently, numerous articles about changes in consumer behavior mention time saving as a key factor. Direct marketing has emphasized the benefits of armchair shopping for years and has much to gain from the time-saving trend.

The need to save time has contributed to the burgeoning growth of non-store sales as opposed to sales through traditional retail outlets. Non-store shopping includes telephone and mail orders to traditional retail outlets; in-home, credit-card-only purchases; direct response purchases in all media, and—coming up fast on the outside—*purchases made through experimental two-way television.* "People are becoming psychologically prepared for new forms of shopping," say marketing professors Larry J. Rosenberg and Elizabeth C. Hirschman in an article in the July 1980 issue of *Harvard Business Review.* They found evidence to indicate that there are enough consumers to support telecommunications marketing which, in their words, is "a virtual certainty with only its period of implementation subject to conjecture."

Rosenberg and Hirschman see the saving of time as the principal consumer benefit in the switch-over to telecommunications shopping. They describe the period when stores traditionally served as the primary distributors for retail products as a time when "the value of consumers' money exceeded the value of their time." This has clearly changed, and the emergence of interactive television is part of that change. Moreover, as that shopper of shoppers, the American woman, enters the work force in greater numbers, shopping that saves time becomes increasingly necessary.

Businesspeople tend to play up the bright side of saving time, stressing the additional benefits, choices, and options it will bring the consumer. But anyone concerned with the psychology of advertising has to look behind that ballyhoo. Why do Americans feel that there isn't enough time to shop, to be entertained, enlightened, and fulfilled even though they *do* in fact have considerable discretionary time? Could it be that it's not just the feeling that there isn't enough time to do all that we like, but the feeling that time itself is running out? People in this country are haunted by an entire cavalry troop of apocalyptic horsemen. Fear breathing down our necks makes us feel the time squeeze ever more strongly. The nostalgia craze, which attempts to neutralize time present by looking back at time past, is a symptom of the national depression. The need to save time in the future is the other side of the coin.

The value of "me time" is rated high by Americans and has been seen as an indication of a reversal of the "things-first, people-second" culture. Citing the May 1977 Harris Survey in an article on "The Time Buying Consumer" in the Winter 1979 *Journal of Retailing,* Leonard L. Berry notes that

> . . . 76 percent of a national sample indicated a preference for "learning to get pleasure out of non-material experiences," rather than for "satisfying our needs for goods and services." . . . Feeling good both mentally and physically is valued, and yet feeling good takes time—time that is taken away from other activities.

Whether we are becoming a less materialistic, "people-first" culture or are just very afraid that time is running out, saving time will be central to the future of marketing. Saving time is already characteristic of both direct marketing and interactive communications, and this has set the stage for their inevitable union and the national importance of that union.

Television provides cheap entertainment and information for people who value their time. The greater the value that is placed on time, the faster we are likely to see television become interactive, putting viewers into immediate and direct contact with data processing systems belonging to social, political, and commercial institutions of all kinds. If television is the future of direct marketing and the future of television is cable, it follows that interactive developments at the end of the rainbow is the pot of gold that both will share.

The Wired City

Groundwork for the interactive revolution was carried out in 1967 when Rand Corporation members H. J. Barnett and E. A. Greenberg published a paper called "A Proposal for Wired City Television." Barnett and Greenberg were looking for ways to obtain more diversified television services. They concluded that the answer might be a broadband cable distribution system similar to the CATV systems of their day but considerably more sophisticated. The result would be "the wired city"—a network of cable connections interactively linking homes and switching centers. A wired city would rely on nothing other than the cable technology of the late 1960s and would be flexible enough to incorporate other systems such as television facsimile.

The "wired city" means that *anyone* can be connected with *anything* within the network—instantly and interactively. This *anything* includes local retailers and national distributors, news and weather bureaus, the stock exchange, banks, city hall, hospitals, police and fire departments, universities, libraries, archives, electronic amusement centers, the post office, and a person's place of work. Home computer terminals within the network would provide people with unlimited opportunities for the storage, retrievable access, analysis, and other uses of data.

Two-way television is made possible by the bidirectional cable that carries signals to and from the TV set. However, in spite of a 1972 FCC ruling that cable systems in this country should be constructed with two-way capabilities, most of the cable currently in use is a one-way street. A second cable would have to be laid to make the hookup interactive. Telephone lines can also carry signals to and from computerized televisions in the home. Laser technology using fiber optics has infinitely multiplied the ability of both cable and telephone lines to carry signals. Experiments with cable and two-way cable television have been going on for decades. Before the interactive revolution began in earnest in the second half of the 1970s, there had been limited applications of interactive systems in schools, hospitals, government offices, and several corporations.

Retail purchases through wired-city interactive television

would be made possible by Electronic Funds Transfer (EFT). In this complex process, electronic impulses, rather than specie or paper drafts or credit-card transactions, form the medium of exchange. Hard cash as we know it never changes hands with EFT. Transactions occur when the necessary data are supplied as computer input. As a result, consumers save time; they needn't write checks. Recipient companies and banks save money through the reduced costs of processing EFT transactions as opposed to processing checks or credit cards. That old nemesis of direct marketers, bad debt, will be greatly reduced.

The 1979 *DM/MA Fact Book on Direct Response Marketing* notes that EFT

> . . . is expected by many experts to evolve into the dominant payment method within the next decade. For example, Arthur D. Little, Inc., Cambridge, Massachusetts, the noted research and consulting firm, has estimated that EFT transactions will represent 17 percent of all transactions by 1980 and 70 percent of all transactions by 1990.

QUBE and Prestel—Two Interactive Systems

Interactive television has been developing seriously for several years in half a dozen European countries, plus Japan, Canada, and the United States. However, the United States has lagged behind in some areas of interactive development, which could be a serious mistake if the electronic information revolution occurs faster than we expect and makes us dependent upon other countries for the technology and equipment we need to keep pace. If our cities are not wired as fast as those of our global neighbors, we stand as much chance of staying on top as one would have trying to win the Indy 500 with a horse and buggy.

Two interactive systems, which are currently in high gear, are particularly important to the future of direct marketing and its advertising. They are the British Post Office's electronic facsimile system, Prestel, and America's QUBE, owned and operated by the mergered Warner Cable Corporation and American Express (Warner/Amex). Prestel was formerly called Viewdata until that name became generic for the use of telephone lines or cable to transmit static pages of data consisting of words, numbers, and simple illustrations to computerized television receivers. QUBE can be used for facsimile transmission, but it is primarily a full-motion medium, exactly like the television we all know, but interactive. (The name "QUBE," incidentally, doesn't mean anything in particular. According to one of its spokespersons, it's just a "catchy, made-up name.")

The QUBE System

QUBE is America's most sophisticated interactive system, and its advertising potential is tremendous. It has been operating in Columbus, Ohio, where the market is slightly younger and more upscale than most markets, but which nevertheless presents a typical cross-section of American values, attitudes, opinions, and buying patterns. In its first six months of operation in 1978, it attracted some 30,000 subscribers, and it is presently expanding services to include Cincinnati and Houston.

QUBE is a living experiment in the television of tomorrow— a preview of the ultimate environment for direct marketing, although it is not yet heavily commercial. As Gustave Hauser, the chairman of Warner Cable, describes it:

> [QUBE is] changing the meaning of what television is. . . . We have taken cable and made it a two-way street. We can send video down the cable and subscribers can send data back up. The five buttons the QUBE subscriber has on the right side of his control box really let him participate in the medium of television for the first time. He can decide which of thirty channels he wants to watch. He can take tests such as the SAT preparatory exams . . . he can participate in a town meeting . . . the QUBE subscriber can also order merchandise or take college classes via television and "talk" with the teacher.

The QUBE control box, or "console," is linked by a thin cable to a computer terminal about the size of a dictionary installed near the TV set. Eighteen buttons on the box allow the viewer to participate in television as never before. Three at the bottom let the subscriber select the service he wants to watch: the premium service consisting only of movies and entertainment specials, community programming, or ordinary network and local television. Ten buttons on the left serve as channel selectors. But the special buttons are the five on the right side of the box, which allow subscribers to send signals back to QUBE's central computers that scan every QUBE household every six seconds. Computer scanning records whether sets are turned off or on and what they are tuned to. It is the kind of interactive monitoring that threatens to make today's Nielsen and Arbitron rating systems obsolete.

Pushing buttons, or something like it, stands to be the big

difference between what people do with their television sets now and what they will do with them tomorrow. "We find that people like to be involved with television beyond watching it," says Gustave Hauser. "Maybe it is a response to loneliness, but they seem to welcome being asked questions they can answer by pushing buttons." Someday even the buttons will be eliminated, and the viewer-TV marriage will be consummated as it is in the Jules Feiffer cartoon of the man who converses with his TV set. People will only have to speak into their television sets to make a direct response purchase or register an opinion. Voice analysis data banks at the central computers will verify whether or not the person speaking is the subscriber registered with the particular interactive system. Your voice will be your fingerprint and credit card.

QUBE subscribers respond to questions on everything from sports to politics. A touch of a button is all it takes to pick a football play or criticize a president. An announcer asks questions either on or off camera, then the screen flashes the message, *Touch now*. Subscribers touch their buttons, and their opinions go back down the cable to a QUBE computer where they are recorded and analyzed. Seconds later, the outcome, broken down into percentages, is reported back on the screen. For instance, when participating subscribers were asked for their opinions immediately following a speech by President Jimmy Carter on America's energy future, viewers learned in a flash that 61 percent of them felt optimistic, 18 percent were pessimistic, and 21 percent were confused. The breakdown corresponded dramatically with a larger sample of Americans later polled through conventional methods.

One QUBE subscriber, who probably typifies many others, was quoted as seeing interactive television as a means of expressing his own ego, of giving him a sense of power and "a sense of directing something far away." This feeling of "counting" and of being in control will influence the form and content of advertising on interactive television. Although advertising doesn't amount to much on today's pay-cable QUBE, as product programming it is likely to be a basic part of interactive television in the future. By definition, advertising on interactive television will be interactive. It will be direct response advertising in new clothes and will take its character from the audience for which it is intended, from people who want to feel in control

Advertising for the participatory medium of interactive television will encourage participation. And it is reasonable to assume that when people feel they count and have choices, the excessive and annoying aspects of today's advertising may be driven out by public opinion that would be more potent in the interactive future. Tomorrow's interactive advertising may be as spare and economized as the future toward which it is heading. In fact, it may be hard to distinguish advertising from pure information. Although we don't know what interactive advertising will look like, commercials now on QUBE may presage what is coming.

Today in Columbus, local merchants use QUBE to sell directly and to get sales leads. The commercials can't hold a candle to the creativity and production values in prime-time network advertising, but, being innovative, they are important and may point to a new wave of advertising not long from now. Consider the commercial for the Bradford Travel Service. Bradford's commercial begins by asking viewers to touch buttons according to their preference for more information about tours to London, Paris, Hawaii, or Rome. In seconds the screen reports that 52 percent of the respondents preferred Paris, and for the following five minutes viewers see a travelogue of the City of Lights. (A slightly more sophisticated system would allow each viewer to see the travelogue of his or her choice.) People who then want more information about Bradford's Parisian Christmas tour are invited to push a second button. The screen thanks them for their response, and within 24 hours a Paris tour package brochure arrives by mail with a request for a $200 deposit.

In another commercial that may foreshadow things to come, a local restaurant offered Christmas gift certificates in denominations ranging from five to twenty dollars. The restaurant got 34 requests for certificates when subscribers pushed a button allowing QUBE's computers to release their names and addresses for billing. The restaurant went on to consider using QUBE to take dinner reservations, with viewers choosing their meals in advance from a menu on the screen.

It takes no great stretch of the imagination to see polished, efficient, and nationwide interactive advertising stemming from provincial spots like these. The flexibility of this kind of marketing is incredibly promising. That it may not be cost-efficient right now does not mean that experiments in interactive advertising with a system like QUBE should or will proceed at a snail's pace.

Britain's Prestel

Outside the United States, interactive telecommunication has reached a high level of development with Prestel, which was developed by the British Post Office and is the world's first two-way computer-based information service. Unlike QUBE, Prestel cannot display the moving images we are used to seeing on film and video tape. Instead, Prestel provides information in the form of alphanumeric data and simple diagrams. Its capacity has been recently expanded to display color photographs.

Prestel is one of several videotext systems using telephone lines or television transmitters to carry signals to and from TV sets in the home or office. Others include Britain's ORACLE and Ceefax, Japan's CAPTAIN, France's Antiope and Teletel, and Canada's Telidon. General Telephone and Electronics (GTE) has licensed Prestel for United States development, and the Knight-Ridder newspaper chain is experimenting with an ambitious interactive telephone-based system in Miami.

When it was first made available as a public service in 1979, Prestel offered 150,000 pages of information in 1,000 categories. That capacity jumped to a quarter of a million pages in less than a year. With Prestel, a screen full of printed information is, in fact, a page; and here we have an example of the blurring of distinctions between traditional broadcast and print media we will see more of as electronic information systems become widespread. The Prestel screen isn't just any kind of page, however. The interactive nature of the system makes it a direct response page—an electronic coupon page, as we shall see.

Over 250 suppliers key their information into Prestel's central computers and can update their information at any time. Thus, Prestel's information is always current and always precise, which wouldn't be possible with any form of printed material. Information is provided by the hundreds of organizations that have coventured Prestel with the British Post Office, including Britain's Stock Exchange, Thomas Cook, British Rail, British Airways, the English Tourist Board, Barclay's Bank, and the *Financial Times*.

Britain's two-way information system was designed to serve business and the public. It is easy to operate and uses a remote control unit similar to a pocket computer for selecting information that may be screened on a special receiving set or a standard TV set that has been modified to receive Prestel. Like QUBE's remote unit, the Prestel keypad has a series of numbered buttons. One of the buttons contacts Prestel's central computer. A second calls up a general index of available information. Finding specific information can be time consuming and costly. Prestel charges are like normal telephone charges and are based on the time a subscriber is connected to the system's central computer. To save subscribers money, Prestel has made a concession to the past; it provides a printed directory of the suppliers it lists.

Understandably, Prestel has many business applications. It offers information about leading companies, financial statistics, intercompany comparisons, investment statistics, exporting information, accountancy standards, employment and real estate information, business law, government statistics, and tax guides. Several times a day the stock exchange lists the share prices and price changes, commodity prices, and foreign exchange rates. Most of this information is available to all Prestel subscribers, but certain confidential information is accessible only through "Closed User Group" facilities that provide certain kinds of information only to authorized users.

A lot of Prestel information is useful for both business and the general public. The "Good Food Guide" lets subscribers see restaurant menus in advance and provides restaurant telephone numbers so they can book reservations immediately. Movie and theater guides provide reviews, ticket prices, and show times. Prestel also covers travel arrangements listing boat, train, and plane timetables, hotel guides, details about currency, and visa information. Prestel will even tell you the kind of plug for your electric razor you'll need for where you're going.

In the home, Prestel is a time-saver. Busy mothers can use it to check prices before they go shopping. And, with a facility still being developed known as a "response frame," Prestel will provide complete armchair shopping services. Subscribers will be able to compare prices at home, as well as to order merchandise.

Prestel spokesmen have compared their "response frames" to coupons in direct response print ads—except there's no coupon to fill out and no postage to pay. Subscribers have only to press a few buttons to send ordering information back down the telephone line to the supplier of information who owns the frame. Messages will be received within moments of dispatch.

Prestel hopes to become a mass market medium and is currently aimed at four broad markets: (1) individuals, (2) sets installed at home but paid for by business, (3) sets on business premises, and (4) sets installed in public locations, such as libraries and hotels, many of which will be coin-operated.

In 1980, Prestel was available to about 30 percent of all telephone subscribers in Great Britain. Live demonstrations of the world's first public Viewdata service have been given in over 30 countries around the world, and an information brochure proudly points out that Prestel is so advanced in its technology "that the Germans and Americans are looking to Britain for (videotext) know-how." Prestel has even launched a small international market trial and is planning to install terminals in the United States, Australia, Sweden, Switzerland, the Federal Republic of Germany, and the Netherlands.

For the present, Prestel and QUBE are getting along without

much advertising, and it might seem that these and future interactive systems will hold advertising to a minimum or have none at all because subscribers pay for the system. The opposite is likely to be the case, at least in this country where advertising and television are practically inseparable. Advertising reduces the total cost of television to the public. And just as standard broadcast television became increasingly saturated with advertising as it grew in influence and importance, so might it be with the interactive systems. The big difference between television advertising today and tomorrow will be the difference between the audiences we now have and will have. Also, because today's commercials are everywhere, they really have no one place of their own and seem to usurp the time of the programs that carry them. Commercials will have a distinct and valued place in interactive systems.

Narrowcasting—Serving a Segmented Audience

If people watching QUBE now are anything like interactive viewers will be 20 years from now, we can assume that future audiences are going to be far more critical and active. They will have become accustomed to having things their way (on television), and their ability to exercise an instant veto over what they are watching will have become second nature. They will be more open to advertising because they will have chosen to watch it, or if they didn't choose it, the commercials they are exposed to will at least be in keeping with their special interests. They will pay closer attention to television advertising because they know that it will ask them to make a decision.

The wide range of programs, information, and services offered by interactive cable television will break audiences into distinct interest groups and will provide the kind of segmented market direct marketers dream about. According to *Newsweek,* futurist Alvin Toffler "regards the broadening of the video spectrum as a part of an over-all demassification of the media, in which we move from a few images distributed widely to many images distributed narrowly . . . to *narrowcasting* rather than broadcasting."

Narrowcasting is the ability to send a certain program or service to a particular group of viewers exclusively. QUBE can do this by feeding a "qualifying list" of selected subscribers to its master computer, enabling only those sets on the list to receive the programming so targeted. The qualified narrowcast audiences will be smaller than broadcast markets, but advertisers will be able to reach them in more significant ways because they will be highly specialized. Commercials addressed to such qualified audiences will reflect viewers' interests, unlike today's unwelcome commercial interruptions.

A great many viewers will also watch commercials purely out of choice. When cable becomes preeminent, advertising will flourish—in its place—on home shopper and catalog channels, on product programs, and on local merchants' channels. Viewers will see advertising because they *want* to see advertising, and they'll see it *when* they want to see it.

The Changing Look of Advertising

As viewers call more of the shots, the look of television advertising will change. Commercials will finally be more in keeping with their audience's preferences. Even the term "commercial" and its present 10-, 30-, 60-second, and two-minute formats will have to be discarded. Modern commercials that look polished now will seem quaint and primitive by tomorrow's standards.

If it remains true that viewers value information in their advertising above anything else, we are likely to see advertising on interactive television stressing information and abandoning the hucksterish techniques and approaches that have drawn fire for years. Information will replace hype, unless the viewers of the future prove that they wanted hype all along. Interactive television will be mainly concerned with the exchange of information, and interactive advertising that stresses information might not even look like advertising to modern eyes. Creativity won't stem from pirating values and symbols from our culture and transferring them to goods and services. The most creative advertising on television will be that which explains and describes something in the most compelling way.

If interactive viewers show that information is mainly what they want in advertising, television advertising will no longer need to exploit viewers' senses of inferiority and daydreams that promise success and happiness as it has in the past. Misleading advertising, advertising that distorts cultural values and over-emphasizes material satisfaction, will be replaced by advertising that does what it should have done all along—communicate the qualities of a product to prospective buyers.

The coming age of interactive telecommunications might even see response advertising incorporating its antithesis, consumer advocacy. Interactive systems will develop in the consumer's interest, and consumers will use those systems in their own interest. Future advertising may also take its cues from what is in the consumer's interest. If the coming years will be ones of underabundance as so many people predict, advertising might have to persuade consumers to buy sparingly, carefully, thoughtfully, and it might have to show them how to do it. This ultimately depends on what the public really wants. Advertising is bound to our culture; it is not independent of it.

In the decades ahead, we can expect response television advertising to pass through at least two major phases before it dominates advertising. The first phase, occurring now, will see response television adopting the styles and techniques of general television advertising. In the second phase, it will start to experiment heavily with cable and cable satellite transmission. Eventually it will become the definitive advertising for interactive television, but by this time it might almost be an invisible public servant—just another variety of instantly accessible information in a world of information.

Response television advertising that finally reflects the needs and wishes of its audience will be useful, necessary, and as honorable as the audience for which it is intended. When those of us who sell things are governed by those to whom we sell, we may be able to step out from under the shadow of Saint Jerome's dictum: *Homo mercator vix numquam potest Deo placere*—"The man who is a merchant can seldom if ever please God."

Appendix A
Response TV Agencies

Sometimes it's hard to find an agency that can plan a great response television campaign and produce good-looking commercials that work. Few of the country's thousands of advertising agencies understand direct marketing. Only a handful of those that do know TV creative, TV production, and response broadcast media buying. Most of the response commercials on television have been produced by one or another of only several companies like Wunderman, Ricotta & Kline and A. Eicoff & Company. There's a geographic imbalance, too. Most agencies that handle response television are in New York City or Chicago. The sames goes for independent media buyers, 800-number answering services, and TV commercial production houses.

This lopsidedness makes it difficult for some clients to find agencies. Advertisers with money inevitably wind up being pitched by the same half-dozen large and medium-sized agencies. Clients who aren't all that flush sometimes have to skip television because it doesn't profit agencies to service them. Other clients are rejected because of possible conflicts—when only a few agencies serve many direct marketing accounts, those agencies have to decline new accounts that are similar to existing accounts. Local retailers who have much to gain from TV direct marketing also find it hard to get agency assistance.

A solution to the problem may come from the more numerous small and medium-sized direct marketing agencies that haven't done television yet but want to try their wings. Clients that are willing to grow with these agencies and share the risks of their first flights have much to gain.

The following direct marketing agencies do work in television. They were selected from a great many direct marketing operations for their television expertise or their potential for doing good work on television. Some of these agencies have

159

mastered television and others are hopeful contenders, but all recognize their stake in response television's growth. No attempt has been made to judge their work. That will be best done by you when you see their reels.

The agencies that are listed supplied the information about themselves, so what follows isn't impartial. Other agencies that do television are not included because they prefer it that way, or simply because I overlooked them (for which I apologize).

AYER DIRECT
(A division of N.W. Ayer ABH International)
1345 Avenue of the Americas
New York, New York 10105
(212) 974-7400
Address inquiries to Robert Sawyer, Senior Vice-President

Ayer Direct is an internal direct marketing unit of a big general agency and is headed by a key figure in the development of modern direct marketing, Bob Sawyer. Bob is working hard and fast to make Ayer Direct's response commercials equal to anything on television. This includes conducting agency seminars to give his writers a common script language, an understanding of what's do-able within a budget, and an awareness of the electronic resources available to them.

Ayer Direct wants to find more creative ways to communicate direct marketing sales messages. It is working at developing new formats that will make direct marketing spots entertain, inform, and sell. It is also exploring television support of other media and "using TV to seed other media with transfer devices."

One of Ayer Direct's successes has been its commercial for AT&T "Big Hello" gift certificates. A phone number is introduced early in this 60-second commercial, is integrated into the story line, and is repeated at the close of the spot. It is handled in such a way that it can be easily localized as needed by AT&T companies all over the country.

Other Ayer Direct clients include Pan Am, DuPont, and the United States Army.

BENTON & BOWLES
909 Third Avenue
New York, New York 10022
(212) 758-6200

Address inquiries to Richard Colligan, Director of Direct Marketing

Benton & Bowles was forming a direct marketing partner company when this book was being typeset. That company should be active now, and, as far as response television is concerned, it will have at its disposal the sophisticated computer system for spot time buying its parent company developed. The B&B slogan, "It's not creative unless it sells" could be a direct marketing maxim. It is a slogan that indicates that the general agency and its new direct marketing partners will share a very important point of view.

BOZELL & JACOBS, INC.
One Dag Hammarskjold Plaza
New York, New York 10017
(212) 644-7200
Address inquiries to Mitch Hisiger, Senior Vice-President

Bozell & Jacobs has 13 offices across the United States, and its direct marketing division operates out of four of those offices. Mitch Hisiger, head of the New York office, sees cable becoming the most important medium in the direct marketer's arsenal by 1985.

This agency's innovative "Charmed Life" commercials for Mutual of Omaha used humor to overcome negative feelings toward insurance and generated sales leads in volume for Mutual's sales force.

Other clients include Evelyn Wood Reading Dynamics—Speed Reading Seminars, Art Instruction Schools, and Club Med.

CHITTICK EGAN ADVERTISING
111 Presidential Boulevard
Balla Cynwyd, Pennsylvania 19004
(215) 667-9600
Address inquiries to William F. Egan, President

Chittick Egan has been Philadelphia's major direct response agency for more than 25 years. It regards television as the most dynamic medium in the future of direct marketing.

The agency has been highly successful with its "Student Life" commercial for Germantown Life Insurance, which generated requests for more than 2,000 booklets in the greater Philadelphia market alone.

Television clients include American Integrity Insurance, Edmund Scientific, the Magna Seal Corporation, Evans Products, and Perfect Photo, Inc.

COMPTON DIRECT MARKETING
625 Madison Avenue
New York, New York 10022
(212) 753-5855
Address inquiries to Jack Brandvein, Creative Director

Compton Direct offers total direct response marketing services in all media.

CUNDALL/WHITEHEAD ADVERTISING, INC.
3000 Bridgeway
Sausalito, California 94965
(415) 332-3625
Address inquiries to Robert Whitehead

Cundall/Whitehead specializes in direct response advertising. TV clients include West Coast Life Insurance and the Willows Shopping Center.

DIAL MEDIA, INC.
59 West Shore Road
Warwick, Rhode Island 02889
(401) 738-5100
Address inquiries to David V. Crocker or Arthur D. Schiff

Dial Media, Inc., is a full-service advertising agency that is doing classic direct response TV demonstrations with more verve and gusto than practically anyone else today. Dial is the one that opens its commercial for Armourcote pots and pans by dropping a raw egg on a delicate hand wearing a diamond ring. "You can't cook on a diamond," says the voice-over, and goes on to introduce non-stick Armourcote.

Dial knows how to grab and hold your attention. Above all it knows how to demonstrate products and structure offers in a way that makes it hard for viewers to pass up the bargain.

Dial's booming sales and creative awards prove, again, that knowing how and when to demonstrate is the backbone of direct response television. Armourcote Cookware, having sold 1,500,000 units to date, is one of the all-time sales leaders among television products. Other Dial success stories include commercials for Ginsu Products and LustreWare, Inc. The agency has also created products for International Broadcast Industries, Inc. (Miracle Painter, Miracle Slicer, Claudette Louberge Pantyhose), and the DuraSteel Corporation of America.

A. EICOFF & COMPANY
520 North Michigan Avenue
Chicago, Illinois 60611
(312) 944-2300
Address inquiries to Alvin Eicoff, President

A. Eicoff & Company is a direct marketing pioneer that aired its first commercial for the Grant Company in 1947. This agency is responsible for what must surely be one of the longest running commercials in TV history—the John Williams "Great Moments in Music" spot for Vista Marketing.

Alvin Eicoff reports, "I was the second person ever to put a direct marketing commercial on television and preceded Charles Antell and National Vitamin. It is our concepts such as the two-minute commercial, the 'Theory of Sales Resistance,' the 'isolation factor,' etc., that have set the standard for the entire television industry.

"It was A. Eicoff & Company in conjunction with the Television Advertising Bureau (TVB), that did the pioneering work responsible for converting many metropolitan stations to opening up direct marketing periods. Jointly we put together the presentation that converted Columbia House, Time-Life, *Reader's Digest,* Playboy, Mattel, etc., to the use of television for direct marketing.

"We pioneered and have more research on support advertising than all other agencies combined. We were responsible for moving the support theory from a percentage of primary media's budget to a scientific variable rating point system."

Over the years, A. Eicoff & Company has created more than 2,000 commercials for a small army of direct marketing clients. The list includes National Liberty Mutual Insurance, Fingerhut, *Reader's Digest,* Meredith Publishing, Doubleday, *Playboy,* Hearst Publishing, GRI, AAA, Amoco Motor Club, Columbia

House, the Longines Symphonette, Mattel, Polygram Records, Cosmetique, Union Fidelity Insurance, Animal Protection Institute, *Newsweek,* and Time-Life Books.

THE FIDLER GROUP, INC.
801 Second Avenue
New York, New York 10017
(212) 611-9230
Address inquiries to Roy Fidler, President, or Sandy Clark, Executive Vice-President

The Fidler Group specializes in bringing its clients creative, control-shattering work in mail and print by the best free-lancers in the business—Bill Jayme, Linda Wells, et al. In 1981, Fidler applied its uncompromising creative standards to television for the first time, and produced an impressive two-minute direct response commercial for *Business Week.* It is an agency that bears watching, and Fidler may wind up producing some of the breakthroughs in response television this book anticipates. The Fidler Group is particularly well-versed in circulation promotion in all media.

FOOTE, CONE & BELDING
200 Park Avenue
New York, New York 10163
(212) 880-9000
Address inquiries to John O'Toole, President

FCB is a well-known, full-service general agency that offers direct response advertising as well. The emphasis here is on "person-to-person" advertising which, like direct marketing, tries to appeal to an individual. The people at FCB believe that advertising is a substitute for a personal sales call and that each prospect must be appealed to as a person, and not as part of a mass audience.

Creative Director Ted Littleford says, "TV direct marketing is becoming increasingly more sophisticated. Once associated with Vegamatics and pop record offers, it has moved into the area of magazine subscriptions and book clubs. With the growth of cable, satellite, and two-way systems like QUBE, TV marketing is not just going to be a factor, it's going to be a way of life."

Clients include Sears, Lifesavers, Clairol, the Government of

Bermuda, Arnold Bakers, British Airways, Emigrant Savings Bank, *Newsweek,* Western Electric, Doubleday, Frito-Lay, and the Boy Scouts of America.

GREY DIRECT MARKETING GROUP, INC.
777 Third Avenue
New York, New York 10017
(212) 557-7180
Address inquiries to George S. Wiedemann, President

A full-service direct marketing agency with consumer accounts and business-to-business accounts, Grey Direct stresses strategy disciplines and media integration.

Grey Direct's President, George Wiedemann, sees television as "still one of the smaller mediums in direct marketing, but it is growing very quickly. As telephone service becomes more sophisticated, the two-minute direct television market will continue to grow. But support is where the true growth potential lies because it is the support mode of television that makes a direct marketer into a Procter & Gamble-type television marketer. Communications technology will bring us a whole new form of interactive television. When that arrives, this medium will surpass all others as the most powerful direct marketing medium."

Grey Direct television clients include *Science 80* magazine, *Outdoor Life,* Kroy Industries, and the Direct Mail/Marketing Association. Grey Direct staffers have formerly worked with Time, Incorporated, magazines, Time-Life Books, *Geo* magazine, the Credit Card Service Bureau, and the Spiegel Catalog Corporation.

HARBOR ASSOCIATES
67 River Road
Cos Cob, Connecticut 06807
(203) 661-2595
Address inquiries to Alan Cartoun or Sheila James

Harbor Associates is a creative/production consultancy headed by former Longines Symphonette Society principals. Sheila James and Alan Cartoun know how to structure a traditional, hard-hitting TV pitch, and they are adept at getting credit card orders for products costing more than twenty dollars.

Familiar direct response commercials by Harbor Associates include spots for the Domino Watch, Shepherd's Coat, Wok, Bamboo Steamer, Safari Bag, Liquid Eraser, and the Salvation Army.

JAMESON ADVERTISING, INC.
750 Third Avenue
New York, New York 10017
(212) 667-2323
Address inquiries to Austin Ettinger, President, or Ed Krauss, Senior Vice-President

Most of this full-service agency's income comes from direct marketing, which allows it to negotiate low broadcast rates for its clients. Jameson clearly sees the promise of future developments in telecommunications to direct marketing, and he anticipates TV time costing less as a result of the proliferation of cable television.

Jameson has done commercials for *Scientific American, Natural History* magazine, the Early American Life Society, and *Country Living,* to mention a few of its direct response accounts. It is particularly proud of its commercial for *Prevention* magazine which pulled in orders at a lower cost per order than print or mail.

LaBUICK & ASSOCIATES
666 North Palm Canyon
Palm Springs, California 92262
(714) 320-7305
Address inquiries to Ed or Faye LaBuick.

Through television, the LaBuicks have sold such products as records, knives, watches, cookware, insurance, magazines, schools, health and beauty aids, jewelry, exercise kits, massage chairs, beds, and tools.

MARCOA DIRECT ADVERTISING, INC.
10 South Riverside Plaza
Chicago, Illinois 60606
(312) 454-0660
Address inquiries to David Hefter, President

Marcoa Direct is a full-service direct response and sales promo-tion agency skilled in broadcast advertising. Marcoa Direct advises that proper testing is the key to successful direct response television and warns clients who are using television for the first time to guard against following general advertising methods.

The agency has created television advertising for World of Beauty, United Equitable Insurance, Heath Kit, and other cli-ents. A Marcoa traffic-building commercial for Mercury Marine outboard motors produced thousands of toll-free inquiries and millions of dollars in sales.

McCANN-ERICKSON MARCH, INC.
485 Lexington Ave.
New York, New York 10017
(212) 286-0460

McCann-Erickson March, Inc. offers a combination of consumer advertising and direct marketing experience for clients that want to launch new product lines, expand share of market, increase response, create a new market image, improve distribution, or reduce cost per sale. The agency has played a pioneering role in the development of direct response broadcast advertising and has consistently come up with fine commercials.

This medium-sized agency has developed effective, economi-cal ways to make broadcast work in support of campaigns in other media. It has proved repeatedly that well-planned combina-tions of broadcast and print or direct mail can sharply upgrade the results produced by each individually.

Over the years it has produced everything from 10-second spots to an entire series of 15-minute programs. It offers the ability to test, analyze, and interpret response to increase the overall efficiency of a total advertising schedule.

Among the clients that have come to value the agency's multimedia marketing expertise are Publishers Clearing House, *Changing Times* magazine, *Newsweek,* the Record Guild, The Margrace Corporation, *Consumer Reports,* Unity Buying Service,

RCA Music Service, *Field & Stream, Mechanics Illustrated, U.S. News & World Report, New Shelter, Cuisine,* and the New York State Lottery.

OGILVY & MATHER DIRECT RESPONSE
675 Third Avenue
New York, New York 10017
(212) 986-6900
Address inquiries to J. W. Pickholz, President

Ogilvy & Mather Direct Response is an international direct response agency with 13 offices in ten countries billing about $80 million worldwide. In New York City alone, the agency employs 150 people and bills close to $50 million.

Creative Director Stanley Winston sees the value of cable as providing almost as precise audience segmentation as mail and print allow. By the end of this century, Winston says, "direct marketing, retailing, and advertising will have changed more dramatically than any time since the advent of television."

O&M Direct recently created an exceptional commercial that outpulled the control commercial by 300 percent. It featured Arnold Palmer encouraging golfers to join the U. S. Golf Association and was done with a minimum of money and a star who was available for only three hours, rain or shine.

O&M Direct's television clients also include Nationwide Insurance; Sears Credit Card Marketing; Time, Incorporated; Canadian Olympic Coins; Nationwide Law; and Burpee.

RAPP & COLLINS, INC.
475 Park Avenue South
New York, New York 10016
(212) 725-8100
Address inquiries to Ed Nash, Executive Vice-President

Rapp & Collins is a full-service direct marketing agency specializing in direct response advertising in all major media. It is proving that television is not only a highly successful way to market products directly and generate qualified leads, but that it is also an extremely economical way to do so.

A successful Rapp & Collins commercial for the apartment complex, Starrett City, used real people to talk about life at Starrett City. Consequently, apartments were rented four times faster than through print and at half the cost.

A persuasive commercial for *Bon Appétit* magazine used sounds and beautiful photographs to evoke the aromas of foods. The subscriptions obtained cost 30 percent to 60 percent less than those obtained through other media, including direct mail.

Rapp's "Save the Children" commercial marked the first time that a child sponsorship organization asked for orders on television and got them—at less cost than in print media. (A sponsor's commitment, incidentally, is a big $400.)

A commercial for *Games* magazine captured the fun of the product and was 50 percent more successful than the print version. Another commercial, for *Consumer Reports,* took a successful but complicated print offer and transferred it to television with even greater success.

Rapp & Collins is owned by Doyle Dane Bernbach, the agency many consider the most creative television agency ever. The Doyle Dane influence should prove to be salutary.

RUSS REID COMPANY
80 South Lake Avenue, Sixth Floor
Pasadena, California 91101
(213) 449-6100
Address inquiries to Russ Reid, President

Russ Reid is a full-service advertising agency specializing in nonprofit religious and cause-related organizations. The agency has created numerous fund-raising spots for various clients in addition to a three-hour show for UNICEF, a two-hour show for Children's Village, and the Campus Crusade for Christ's "I Found It!" campaign.

Most of its programming is of a telethon nature, and the agency claims that its telethons are currently raising more money than any other telethons on the air. Reid feels that effective fund-raising television will require more and more tightly produced programming. "As costs go up," he says, "programs will become shorter, requiring finely tuned offers to increase efficiency."

SCHEIN/BLATTSTEIN ADVERTISING
420 Madison Avenue
New York, New York 10017
(212) 758-1555
Address inquiries to E. Schein, President

This full-service agency specializes in magazine circulation promotion and product marketing and development, as well as educational and financial services. It is interested in the possibilities that pay-TV might allow for split-testing commercials prior to roll-out.

Technical Career Institutes, *Jewish Living* magazine, and Sanford C. Bernstein & Company Investment Managers are several of the agency's television clients. Schein/Blattstein is particularly pleased with its "How Did I Get This Great Career" commercial, which consistently produces low lead and order costs and has outpulled six other spots.

SCHWAB/BEATTY
A division of Marsteller, Inc.
866 Third Avenue
New York, New York 10022
(212) 752-6500
Address inquiries to Benson Bieley, Account Supervisor

Established in 1922, Schwab/Beatty is the oldest agency specializing in direct response advertising. Television clients include Corinthian Mint; Littleton Coin Company; Natpac, Inc.; and Walter J. Black Book Clubs.

SHELDON COMMUNICATIONS, INC.
274 Madison Avenue
New York, New York 10016
(212) 889-4422
Address inquiries to Sheldon Hechtman, President

Sheldon Communications is a time-buying service specializing in direct response broadcast advertising. It frequently uses leading independent creative suppliers and can provide its clients with full direct response broadcast creative services.

Sheldon Hechtman believes that television's future is now. Characterizing the technological revolution in television, CATV, and satellite TV as "mind-boggling," Hechtman cites more stations to view, greater audience segmentation, and more opportunities for direct marketers than ever.

Clients include *Newsweek, Inside Sports,* Xerox Educational Publications, ABC Leisure Magazines, Johnson Publications, Hannover House, *Essence* magazine, Elm City Photo, *Parents*

Magazine, Laurie's Records, and Blaine Worthington Enterprises.

SOSKIN/THOMPSON
A division of J. Walter Thompson Company
655 Madison Avenue
New York, New York 10021
(212) 421-6073
Address inquiries to David Soskin, President

David Soskin, president of the direct marketing arm of J. Walter Thompson Company, sees tremendous potential in cable and interactive television. He believes that electronic funds transfer will make ordering and subscribing through television much easier by eliminating the bad debt factor. Soskin feels that support television, especially in cable, will make direct response television a mass medium, yet a selective one.

Television clients include the Sierra Club, 20th Century Fox, and the Video Club of America.

MAXWELL SROGE COMPANY, INC.
303 East Ohio Street
Chicago, Illinois 60611
(312) 266-4900
Address inquiries to Maxwell Sroge or A. Fishman

This leading direct marketing agency specializes in mail-order business development, consulting, and advertising. It is experienced in the start-up and pilot management of major mail-order businesses.

For Sroge, the increasing cost of other media make the future of response television bright indeed. The agency believes that the integrated use of television with other media proves highly cost-efficient and that interactive cable will contribute to a growth explosion.

Television clients include Bell and Howell Schools, Polymusic, Mattel, Mister Rogers, and Longines. Sroge's record club concept, Music Scene, swamped the client with orders. Its work with Bell and Howell helped build the largest vocational home-study school. The well-known commercial for Popeil's Pocket Fisherman sold millions of units and was created by Sroge's TV creative director when he was at another agency.

WILLIAM STEINER ASSOCIATES, INC.
135 East 55th Street
New York, New York 10022
(212) 688-7030
Address inquiries to Ms. Lee Livingston, Vice-President

The full-service direct marketing agency of William Steiner Associates provides counsel, planning, and creative services for clients in all direct response media. The agency has been serving a sizable roster of advertisers for the past 30 years. Steiner Associates uses a team of 35 copywriters and specialists on a "stringer basis," thereby offering its clients the services of many of the top pros in the field.

The agency is particularly proud of its commercials for the Apex Technical School, which were designed to get qualified inquiries for air conditioning and refrigeration courses. Its selection of TV stations and programs was a major factor in getting the required number of inquiries and conversions for the $1,500 course.

STONE & ADLER
A Young & Rubicam Company
150 North Wacker Drive
Chicago, Illinois 60606
(312) 346-6100
Address inquiries to Jim Rose

Stone & Adler is a Young & Rubicam company specializing in direct marketing advertising in all media. Chairman Robert Stone is a legendary figure in the business and literally wrote the book on successful direct marketing methods.

The agency's affiliation with Y & R promises to lead to more creative and arresting commercials. The combination of the country's largest general agency and this most distinguished direct marketing agency should prove powerful and effective.

Stone & Adler's television credits include commercials for Oak Communications, the ChemLawn Corporation, *U.S. News & World Report,* plus support campaigns for Montgomery Ward, Ambassador Leather, and Science Research Associates' Plant Care continuity program. The agency is especially proud of its effective television compaigns for Oak Communications and ChemLawn.

TLK DIRECT MARKETING
605 Third Avenue
New York, New York 10016
(212) 972-9000
Address inquiries to David Henneberry, Senior Partner

Tatham-Laird and Kudner Direct Marketing is a major direct response marketing, consulting, and advertising agency of long standing. For a long time, its best known client was the RCA Music Service for whom the agency has produced a number of commercials.

Other TLK direct marketing clients using television include *World Book Encyclopedia,* National Liberty Insurance, the Franklin Mint, Greater New York Savings Bank, the Deltona Corporation, and the Polygram Corporation.

PETER VANE ADVERTISING
274 Madison Avenue
New York, New York 10016
(212) 679-8260
Address inquiries to Peter or Penny Vane

This fast-growing direct response agency specializes in every aspect of direct marketing including research, drafting marketing plans, and creative advertising in direct mail, print, and broadcast.

THE FRANK VOS COMPANY
485 Madison Avenue
New York, New York 10022
(212) 371-5100
Address inquiries to Thomas J. Turner, Executive Vice-President

Frank Vos has been active in direct marketing for many years, formerly as part of Vos & White and prior to that with Altman, Vos and Reichberg.

The Vos Company has done commercials for Xerox Education Publications ("Popcorn Bag," "Sweet Pickles," "I Can Read"), the Creative Learning Program, and the Illustrated Wildlife Treasury Program. There are also Vos commercials for Amazoy Zoysia Grass and Fingerhut's "Great Impressions" apparel.

WUNDERMAN, RICOTTA & KLINE, INC.
A Young & Rubicam Company
575 Madison Ave.
New York, New York 10022
(212) 752-9800
Address inquiries to Mike Slosberg, President

Wunderman, Ricotta & Kline, Inc., is the world's largest full-service agency devoted to direct marketing. It maintains 17 offices around the world and billed approximately $179 million in 1980. For many years the guiding light of the agency has been its founder, Lester Wunderman, who is responsible for numerous direct marketing milestones.

The acquisition of WRK by its parent agency, Young & Rubicam, increased its scope and upgraded its creative product. (Young & Rubicam, interestingly, is the agency most concerned with exploring advertising on cable television.)

This large, specialized, and efficient agency is responsible for producing hundreds of direct response and support commercials yearly. Its clients cover the entire direct marketing spectrum—from magazines, catalog operations, continuity programs, to off-page general merchandise, crafts, and couponing. Clients include *Time* magazine, *Fortune, Sports Illustrated,* New York Telephone's Dial-A-Joke, the Dow Jones Report and other telephone services, Vista Marketing, Time-Life Books, General Foods, Harlequin Books, Merrill Lynch, Johnson & Johnson, the Columbia Record and Tape Club, and many others.

WRK has an excellent track record for commercials that work and employ high levels of strategic and executional values. The agency places a premium on creative excellence and has the awards to prove it.

Credit for leading WRK into the 1980s goes to President Mike Slosberg, who reflects the linkup between consumer advertising and direct marketing better than almost anyone else. He was with Young & Rubicam for 18 years before he was given the job of running Wunderman, and the experience of those years shows in WRK's polished commercials.

WUNDERMAN, RICOTTA & KLINE, LA, INC.
3435 Wilshire Boulevard
Los Angeles, California 90010

(213) 736-7400
Address inquiries to James M. Stetler, Senior Vice-President

This is the West Coast branch of Wunderman, Ricotta & Kline.

Appendix B
Broadcast Planning Decisions

by Barbara Lewis
Vice-President and Director of Media Services
McCann-Erickson March, Inc.

Viability of Broadcast Direct Response

To determine which direct response medium has the greatest sales potential, several factors must be considered:

- THE OFFER—How expensive is the product? Generally, higher-priced items are not successful with broadcast advertising because the viewer wants to know more about the product than can be given in a 120-second commercial. If it is a high-cost product, television or radio can be utilized in a two-step process: use electronic media to generate inquiries and convert to sale by direct mail or sales follow-up. A one-step sale will probably be more successful with direct mail, newspaper, or magazine advertising.
- CREATIVE—Does the product need the visual advantage that television can provide? Will radio sell the product without the visual stimulus? Will a great deal of copy be required to sell the product?
- COST—Compare each medium in terms of necessary sales volume in relation to the acceptable order cost to determine which medium offers the greatest efficiency.

Many advertisers who had previously utilized other direct response media have found that broadcast direct sell marketing increases response dramatically at a much more efficient cost. Very seldom, however, will an advertiser release actual figures

177

supporting this, since it is a highly competitive market. Broadcast, however, will not work successfully for every product, but if you consider the efficiencies of television compared to other direct response media, it becomes quickly apparent why television can be utilized more efficiently in many cases.

MEDIA COSTS

Media	Avg. CPM
Direct Mail	$250
Newspaper Inserts	25
ROP Newspaper	9
Consumer Magazines	15
Television	3

Every medium can be measured on an equal basis to determine which has the greatest potential. Aside from cost per order, media results can be analyzed by examining response per thousand. The accompanying chart compares potential effectiveness for a hypothetical advertiser. The same method can be applied on a post-buy basis using actual results.

ACCEPTABLE COST PER ORDER: $5.00

SPACE

Publication	Circ. (000)	Cost B/W Page	CPM	Orders/M Circ. @ $5	Total Orders
Saturday Review	530	$ 4,900	$9.25	1.85	980
Smithsonian	1,674	15,000	8.96	1.79	3,000
N.Y. Times	1,400	8,400	6.00	1.20	1,680
Parade	21,200	111,900	5.28	1.06	22,380

TELEVISION

Market	TV HH (000)	Station	Weekly Cost	Orders/M TV HH @$5	Total Orders
Albany	437	WAST	$1,500	0.69	30 0
Albany	437	WTEN	2,500	1.14	500
New York	6,376	WNEW	3,000	0.94	600
St. Louis	972	KPLR	2,000	0.41	400

Thus, we can compare what each medium or advertising vehicle must generate to achieve an acceptable cost per order. If there has been previous experience, past records will indicate whether the projections are realistic in terms of past response rates.

Often, more than one medium has potential for producing efficient response. All things being equal, if creative factors are not a problem, test each medium or combinations of media to see which produces sales more efficiently.

Media Budgets

Direct response budgets are a function of the volume of orders that must be achieved and the acceptable order cost. If advertising must generate 150,000 orders at a maximum cost per order of $3.50, the budget appropriated must be $525,000. Analyze product cost, shipping and operating expenses to determine profitability at various levels of volume to determine how much you can afford to pay for each order.

Test Budgets

Direct response broadcast requires a much smaller budget for testing than general broadcast advertising, since many up-front costs are eliminated, such as consumer and market research and pre-testing of commercials. Unlike general advertising where a test market universe equivalent to 5 percent of total United States households is the accepted standard, direct response offers can be tested much less expensively.

A one-week test in five markets, using about ten spots, can range from $10,000 to $30,000, depending upon the test markets selected. And, each test market will generate revenue, so that most or all of the media costs will be recouped, according to the degree of success of the test program.

Commercial Testing—Market Selection

The fastest and surest way to test a direct sell commercial is also the simplest: run it on-air. While there are many methods of pre-testing a commercial, these research systems can provide only diagnostic data indicating whether the sales points presented will be effective, but they cannot project what actual response will be. There are too many variables when it comes to direct marketing for research of this sort to provide anything more than direction. The cost of pre-testing is generally equivalent to in-market testing, but the in-market test provides hard data from which future sales can be projected.

Select a group of markets, buy a schedule in each market, and run the commercial for a one- or two-week period. According to sales potential, markets should be selected that are representative of the sales universe. If the product has broad national appeal, the test cell should include markets in each area of the country to eliminate any geographical bias. If the product has only limited appeal, test markets should be chosen that are representative of the areas where the greatest sales can be anticipated.

By the end of the test period, almost all the information necessary to analyze and project future campaigns is at hand.

Roll-Out Budgets

Once the initial test program has indicated that the offer is viable at the established cost per order, the number of roll-out markets and projected orders that must be achieved is a marketing decision. Budget, as stated earlier, is based on the sales volume necessary at the maximum acceptable order cost. Market selection should be based on knowledge of where the greatest sales potential lies.

Market Selection

Based on sales records and marketing data, select those television markets that have the greatest sales potential and that have the capacity to produce great volume efficiently. If sales are strong via other marketing methods, for example, in California, examine California television markets.

MARKET	TELEVISION HOUSEHOLDS
Bakersfield	107,040
Chico/Redding	118,820
Eureka	53,800
Fresno	331,400
Los Angeles	4,154,440
Monterey/Salinas	160,120
Sacramento/Stockton	717,370
San Diego	702,600
San Francisco	1,976,300

Obviously there is greater sales potential in Los Angeles than in Eureka and, generally, the larger the market, the lower your schedule costs are on a cost per thousand household basis.

Target Audience

Determine the demographic profile of your prospective customer in terms of sex and age so that programming can be purchased to most effeciently reach that specific target audience.

Demographics: The age, sex, income, and education of the primary consumer.

Psychographics: Lifestyle, behavior, and attitudes of the primary consumer.

The television rating services measure viewing preferences for each television market by program in terms of:

RATING (HOUSEHOLDS)

Household Audiences:

Total Men/Total Women
Age: 18–24
     25–34
     35–49
     50+
     Teens
     Children

Education and income data are available nationally by program. Psychographic data are not measured. Once the demographic profile of your primary prospect has been determined, television can be purchased to deliver the greatest audience against that prospect, thus providing greater efficiency.

Schedule Selection

Because we are interested in generating orders at the lowest possible cost, a great deal of pre-buy analysis should be done before committing to a specific schedule. However, first let us examine the ways in which direct response television can be bought.

ROS—Run-of-Schedule

The station will place the commercial in unsold time. The advertiser can express a preference for specific programs, but the station does not have to honor these requests. A run-of-schedule is generally the lowest cost method of purchasing time and can work very well for a product with broad demographic criteria.

Fixed Position

Time on specific programs can be purchased. Some stations will sell fixed programming at the same price as ROS, others will charge a higher price. (Since the 120-second commercial is the length most often used by direct marketers, discussion will be limited to programming that can carry a two-minute spot.)

With the exception of independent stations, most stations can accept a two-minute spot only in certain areas: in daytime, programs such as "Good Morning, America," "Morning," "Today," and "Phil Donahue" can take these spots. Afternoon movies and syndicated shows like "Mike Douglas," "Hollywood Squares," "Merv Griffin," and the late night vehicles—"CBS Late Movie," "Tonight," "Tomorrow," local movies—all can carry :120s. The independent station, which has no network affiliation, can usually accept a two-minute spot in almost all programs. Each station has different areas where it will put a two-minute commercial, and programs change frequently.

When considering the available programs, first examine them in terms of your demographic target to determine whether program content is compatible with the audience that comprises primary prospects. Avoid programs that have high attentiveness, such as news, since viewer involvement with program content generally means that there will be a lack of viewer involvement with a direct sell commercial.

Examine the cost of individual programs and the total schedule in terms of the acceptable CPO. How many orders must the spot/schedule generate to pay out? A spot that must produce only 10 orders has a greater chance of success than one that must generate 50 orders.

Reach/Frequency

Reach: The number of different homes (or individuals) exposed to a medium within a given period of time, usually one week or four weeks.

Frequency: The average number of commercial messages to which a home (or individual) reached by a schedule is exposed within a given period of time, usually one week or four weeks.

Each advertising medium has a maximum reach potential, as does each television daypart. Prime time has the greatest reach capability, while daytime, early evening, and late night have lower reach potential and greater frequency potential.

The direct marketer need not be concerned with reach and frequency. Unlike a general advertiser who must reach the greatest possible audience with advertising dollars, the direct marketer is only interested in reaching those people who will immediately respond to the offer. Therefore, the total market reach and frequency has no practical application in this narrow universe.

GRP Levels

Ratings are a measurement of audience. Television and radio are surveyed to determined audience viewing/listening preferences. One rating point equals 1 percent of the total market household/specific audience segment.

. With a direct sell proposition, ratings are important only in a negative sense. Because research has shown that there is greater audience attentiveness to high-rated programs, the direct marketer wants to purchase low-rated programming. When a viewer is highly attentive to program content, he will also be attentive to the commercials, but he will not *act* at that time. *He is too involved with the program.*

Conversely, the lower-rated programs that do not have high viewer attentiveness are the areas where we can expect actionable advertising to be successful. If the viewer is involved with the plot of "Dallas," for example, he will not grab pencil and paper or run to the telephone to respond to an offer. The best we can expect is that he will remember the product advertised within the program. But if he is watching the umpteenth rerun of "Lucy" or an old movie, he will not be as attentive to the program, and, in that environment, the chance for positive action to a direct sell commercial is far greater.

Seasonality

Because television and radio rates are based on demand, clearance of two-minute commercial positions is basically limited to twice a year: post-Christmas to March and late June through mid-September. When there is high demand for time by general advertisers, it is much more profitable to a station to sell four 30-second spots rather than one 120-second spot. But when general advertising is soft, the direct response advertiser can buy two-minute spots at very low rates. In high demand periods, in order to buy a two-minute spot, it is likely that the cost will be equivalent to four times the 30-second rate, and it is very unlikely that pay-out would be at an acceptable rate. During the first quarter, viewing levels are at their highest while costs are at their lowest. Therefore, it becomes extremely advantageous to schedule advertising at that time. Summer rates tend to be about 15 percent higher than in the first quarter, but viewing levels are much lower. Still, since there is very little first-run programming, this is a good time for direct response propositions.

Seasonal variations in household TV usage are indexed below by daypart.

	Annual Avg.	1st Quarter	2nd Quarter	3rd Quarter	4th Quarter
Daytime	100	111	88	96	96
Early Fringe	100	117	90	87	107
Prime	100	109	95	91	101
Late Fringe	100	100	92	100	104

Preemptions

Television is a supply and demand medium. An advertiser who is willing to pay a higher price for the spot can preempt another advertiser. Makegoods can be offered by the station. However, a makegood should be accepted only if the schedule is generating orders at an acceptable cost. If results to date are marginal or bad, do not accept a makegood. Save the money to spend where it will increase profitability.

Test Examples/Results Analysis

Before a product is put into the marketplace, the maximum price that can be paid for each order via broadcast must be determined. Analysis of results to determine actual pay-out is a simple mathematical function:

TEST RESULTS ANALYSIS

Cost ÷ Orders = Cost per order (CPO)

Market	Station	Total Expenditure	Total Orders	CPO
A	WXXX	$ 3,000	985	$ 3.05
B	WYYY	1,700	362	4.70
C	KXXX	4,200	647	6.49
D	KYYY	540	45	12.00
E	WZZZ	7,650	2,356	3.25
Total Schedule		$17,090	4,395	$3.89

If the acceptable cost per order was $7.50, it becomes quickly apparent that television produced orders at 48% below the maximum that could be paid and that the product is indeed a viable one that can be marketed profitably across the country.

Schedule Analysis

If telephone orders have been accepted during the test, a great deal of additional information can be compiled to provide direction in terms of where future schedules should be placed to maximize efficiency.

Each television station, along with its invoice, provides an affidavit of performance indicating precisely the time each spot ran. By combining this information with the hour-by-hour response reports from the telephone answering services, analysis will show which programs generated the greatest number of orders at the most efficient cost.

MARKET A—STATION WXXX

Day/Time	Program	Cost Per Spot	Total Orders	CPO
Mon. 4:43PM	Mike Douglas	$275	76	$3.62
Tues. 11:08PM	Late Show	100	26	3.85
Wed. 2:11AM	Late Late Show	50	3	16.67
Thu. 9:26AM	Lucy	225	110	2.05
Thu. 3:40PM	Afternoon Movie	275	95	2.89
Fri. 7:18PM	Match Game	550	80	6.88
Fri. 2:36AM	Late Late Show	50	4	12.50

Future schedules, therefore, should avoid very late night programs and should include a heavy concentration of daytime programming.

Mail vs. Phone

If orders have been accepted by phone and by mail, analysis should be done to determine which method generated the greatest response. If mail response was far greater than telephone response, it perhaps would produce orders at greater efficiency to exclude phone response in the future, or vice versa.

Market	Station	Total Expenditure	Phone	%	CPO	Mail	%	CPO
A	WXXX	$3,000	660	67	$ 4.55	325	33	$9.23
B	WYYY	1,700	152	42	11.18	210	58	8.10

Naturally, without phone response, program efficiency cannot be analyzed. However, heavy mail response generally indicates than an older audience is your primary purchaser and future programs can be selected to reach that audience.

Back-end Analysis

If the offer involves a "Bill Later" or COD arrangement, it is vitally important to determine how much non-pay or COD refusal is involved. If your gross order cost was close to the acceptable CPO and 50 percent of the orders were lost, then what looked like a profitable venture may very well be extremely inefficient.

ACCEPTABLE ORDER COST: $7.50

Market	Station	Total Expenditures	Gross Orders	CPO	Net Orders	% Non-Pay	Net CPO
A	WXXX	$3,000	985	$3.05	758	23	$3.95
B	WYYY	1,700	362	4.70	181	50	9.39
C	KXXX	4,200	647	6.49	582	10	7.22
D	KYYY	540	45	12.00	38	15	14.21
E	WZZZ	7,650	2,356	3.24	1,579	33	4.85
	Total Schedule	$17,090	4,395	$3.89	3,138	29	$5.45

SOURCE: Karen Burns, ed., *Direct Response Broadcast and the New Electronic Media,* DM/MA Information Central Monograph no. 2, © Direct Mail/Marketing Association.

This example indicates that the schedule produced profitably overall on a net basis. However, future schedules would have to generate a *GROSS CPO* of $5.33 to achieve a *NET CPO* of $7.50. ($7.50—29 percent average non-pay.) In addition, Market B would not be utilized again in view of the high incidence of non-pay.

Appendix C
Cable Advertising Costs and Testing

by Robert D. Burgener, Chairman of the Board, Cable Ad Associates

SOURCE: Karen Burns, ed., *Direct Response Broadcast and the New Electronic Media,* DM/MA Information Central Monograph no. 2, © Direct Mail/Marketing Association.

While current National Cable Television Association (NCTA) figures show that only 15 percent of the cable systems in the United States sell advertising time, that figure is growing. At the same time, the cable operator's ability to provide audience demographics for advertisers is also growing. What is certain at this time is that homes with cable television tend to watch more programs than do non-cable homes (approximately 1.3 hours more a day) and the viewers tend to be younger and more up-scale.

The income argument and the "pitch the rich" slogans used by one programmer are accurate for the short term based on the fact that when a franchise is awarded for an entire community, the cable operator logically is going to build in the areas that can best afford the service first and then reach into the other marginal areas. As cable expands to cover the full limits of its franchise requirements, the audience demographics will look more and more like general circulation figures in terms of the *homes using cable*. However, because of cable's narrowcasting techniques of programming, it will still be possible to go back to those figures and pull out the number of subscribers taking sports, religious, or movie program channels.

In the following pages, we will look at a specific buy for a direct marketer and the use of different program services to target specific audiences.

Buying Advertising Time on Cable

There are a number of ways for direct marketers to become involved in cable television. One is to purchase time on the so-called superstations such as WTBS in Atlanta, WGN in Chicago, or WOR in New York City. In this situation, you are buying a regular television schedule of programming with the added distribution provided by satellite to cable systems beyond the normal broadcast reach of that station.

A second option is to purchase network time on one of the advertising-supported program suppliers such as Entertainment/Sports Programming Network (ESPN), USA network, Satellite Programming Network (SPN), or others that are currently vying for transponder (satellite) distribution space. Regional sports and entertainment networks such as the Gill network in the San Francisco Bay area are also being developed. As with the superstations, the program networks provide distribution to a number of markets with traditional 30-second, 60-second, and two-minute advertising positions available.

A final option would be to buy individual markets. Some people have referred to this as buying television by ZIP code. In this case, the direct marketer would attempt to contact and arrange distribution of his commercial within the schedule of the individual system. This system could be carrying cable-originated programming which provides local programming that includes positions for inserting advertising at the local level. At some point, there will no doubt develop specific shopper service channels within each system. The off-air or broadcast signals carried by the cable system may not be altered. Thus, it is not possible for the cable operator to take out a broadcast commercial and insert his own.

Testing Cable Advertising

By using the satellite, it is possible to conduct a national test market. In the case of superstations such as WTBS, which claims coverage in eight million homes, it would be possible for the direct marketer to purchase a traditional schedule, meaning two-minute spots in late-fringe or other typical direct marketing time slots, and to run that schedule for one week. During that week, responses could be measured in specific areas of the country or specific markets identified as strong responders. In this case, the direct marketer hasn't really used anything in cable television that he wouldn't buy in broadcast television except the additional distribution.

In another scenario, a direct marketer with products that would normally be identified with a strong male audience or a sports-enthusiast audience might purchase one of the two sports programming networks, either ESPN or USA network. Each claims distribution to at least five million cable homes. Again, position could be in late-fringe or other so-called direct marketing time slots or specific programs can be purchased. In fact, many of the networks will offer sponsorship for tournaments or other activities. In this case, the narrowcasting concept of appealing only to sports enthusiasts applies.

At this time, the satellite program network, SPN, is the closest cable equivalent to a traditional broadcast network such as ABC, CBS, or NBC, in terms of offering a full day's programming to a variety of audiences, meaning talk shows, financial shows, and movies. The principal differences are that these movies are usually two hours in length, have commercial interruptions at the beginning and end with an intermission, but not the number of breaks that normally occur. This is in keeping with the cable television concept that movies should be free of or with a limited number of commercial interruptions. In this case, the direct marketer could purchase positions and reach that audience that is attracted to this particular feature of cable television. The Satellite Program Network claims a Nielsen Report of four million homes and viewership of two and a half million.

Satellite Delivery to Spot Markets

One of the most exciting aspects of the cable television marketplace is its ability to receive satellite-delivered signals. In the past, with a broadcast station, a direct marketer or any advertiser was required to make copies of his commercial and then send them through the mails or other delivery services to the markets where they would be played. Using the satellite distribution services, it is possible to take a single copy of the commercial and distribute it to many markets where it would be copied at the head end of the cable system. While we have not eliminated the need to make a copy, we have eliminated the postal delivery and all of those intermediate steps of packing, unpacking, and hoping the tape was not squashed in the process. This service now makes it efficient to go to a number of spot markets; in fact, the more markets selected, the more efficient the satellite distribution. At the spot market level, the direct marketer's commercial can then run on whatever national network programs pulled well in that market, plus any other program positions that are negotiated with that local system. In this case, a commercial message that perhaps did not pull well enough in national distribution to justify continued buys on a national network can still enjoy the benefits of satellite distribution to local markets, where it did perform well.

Sample Cable Advertising Plan

Goal: Identify good cable markets for Product X and attempt to increase sales in those markets by adding spot sales.

Method: Purchase cable program networks to blanket country (first flight). Through monitoring of responses from first flight, initiate second flight to include spot markets.

SATELLITE SERVICE	PROGRAM	TIME	EXPOSURES
Flight 1			
SPN	MovieTown	5PM(E) 2PM(W)	2× day 1 wk
ESPN	Tennis	1AM(E) 10PM(W)	4× day 1 wk
Flight 2			
SPN	MovieTown	1PM(E) 10AM(W)	2× day 1 wk
Tulsa, OK	SPN MovieTown	5PM(E)	2× day 1 wk + ROS
Xenia, OH	SPN MovieTown	5PM(E)	4× day 1 wk
Dubuque, IA	SPN MovieTown	5PM(E)	2× day 1 wk + ROS
	Local News	10PM(E)	1× day Tues. Wed. Thur.
San Francisco, CA	ESPN Tennis	10PM(W)	4× per event + ROS Sports

SPN reaches approximately three million homes in 468 markets (systems) at a cost of between \$125 and \$150 per two-minute spot. ESPN reaches up to five million homes in 728 markets (systems) at a cost of \$900 per spot. Taking the SPN example, the cost for delivering the message to each home is .0005 cents (using \$150/spot). In the case of ESPN Sports, the cost is eighteen hundredths of a cent per home (.00018 cents). The cost per order then is determined by the number of those homes that actually call; however, the cost of getting the message there is considerably less expensive using satellite delivered cable programming than by other means.

Who to Call

The National Cable Television Association publishes the *Cable Advertising Directory,* which lists the cable systems that carry advertising (price: \$10.00 from NCTA, 918 16th Street NW, Washington, D.C. 20006). In addition, a number of companies acting as representatives for the sale of cable advertising time have emerged. A good way for direct marketers to determine the viability of the spot cable market is to simply call the city in question, determine if it has a cable system, and contact the manager directly. Rates are usually negotiable.

Of the advertising-supported network program suppliers, USA network and ESPN have in-house sales forces, while SPN uses Eastman CableRep for their ad time sales. Network buys can be made through these program suppliers or through the super-stations.

For individual spot sales, the direct marketer can contact the system and negotiate rates and placement.

Cost for Copies

The principal concern in using the cable system to distribute commercials from the satellite centers is to coordinate the exact time when the commercial will be shown so that the receiving cable operator need not tie up technicians and equipment during odd hours.

When a well-coordinated plan is presented, the charges for making the copy at the system end can be as low as $10 per spot to a maximum of $25. Often, many cable systems will provide this service without charge to advertisers buying regular spot sched-ules.

Appendix D
AICP Studio Cost Summary

Bid estimates for commercials should be presented on this form or on one like it. Just looking at the hundreds of details it breaks out individually encourages appreciation for the producer whose job is to weave loose ends into a perfect whole.

STUDIO COST SUMMARY

Date:

Production Co:	Agency: — Agency job #
Address:	Client: — Product:
Telephone No.: — Job #	
Production Contact:	Agency prod: — Tel:
Director:	Agency art dir: — Tel:
Camerman:	Agency writer: — Tel:
Set Designer:	Agency Bus. Mgr: — Tel:
Editor:	Commercial title: — No. — Length:
No. pre-prod. days — pre-light/rehearse	1.
No. build/strike days — Hours:	2.
No. Studio shoot days — Hours:	3.
No. Location days — Hours:	4.
Location sites:	Agency supplies:

SUMMARY OF ESTIMATED PRODUCTION COSTS				
1. Pre-production and wrap costs				
2. Shooting crew labor				
3. Studio costs: Build / shoot / strike				
4. Location travel and expenses				
5. Equipment costs				
6. Film stock develop and print: No. feet — mm				
7. Props, wardrobe, animals				
8. Payroll taxes, P & W, and misc.				
9. Sub total: Direct costs				
10. Director / creative fees				
11. Insurance:				
12. Mark - up: (% of direct costs)				
13. Editorial and finishing per:				
14. Talent costs and expenses				
15. Total production estimate				
16. Weather day				
17.				
18.				

Comments:

AICP Studio Cost Summary   195

A: PRE-PROD'N / WRAP   B: SHOOTING

CREW	ESTIMATED				(Actual)				ESTIMATED				(Actual)		
	Days	Rate	O/T Hrs	Total	Days	Rate	Total		Days	Rate	O/T Hrs	Total	Days	Rate	Total
1. Producer:															
2. Asst. Director:															
3. Dir. Photography:															
4. Camera Operator:															
5. Asst. Cameraman:															
6. Outside Props:															
7. Inside Props:															
a.															
b.															
c.															
d.															
e.															
8. Electricians:															
a.															
b.															
c.															
d.															
e.															
9. Grips:															
a.															
b.															
c.															
d.															
e.															
10. Mixer (or Playback:)															
11. Recordist:															
12. Boom Man:															
13. Make-Up:															
14. Hair:															
15. Stylist:															
16. Wardrobe Attendant:															
17. Script Clerk:															
18. Home Economist:															
19. Scenics:															
20. VTR Man:															
21. EFX Man:															
22. Nurse:															
23. Telepr. & Operator:															
24. Generator Man:															
25. Still Man:															
26. Loc. Contact/Scout:															
27. P. A.															
28. 2nd A. D.															
29. Teamsters															
a)															
b)															
c)															
30.															
	SUB TOTAL A								SUB TOTAL B						

Job Description / Schedule Breakdown

196 Response Television

PAGE 2

PRE-PRODUCTION & WRAP/MATERIALS & EXPENSES	Estimated	Actual	
31. Auto Rentals (Cars @ $ x days)			
32. Air Fares: No. of people ( ) x Amount per fare ( )			
33. Per Diems: No. of people ( ) x Amount per day ( )			
34. Still Camera Rental & Film			
35. Messengers			
36. Trucking			
37. Deliveries & Taxis			
38. Home Economist Supplies			
39. Telephone & Cable			
40. Art Work			
41. Casting (Days @ $)			
42. Casting Facilities / Equipment			
SUB TOTAL C			

SET CONSTRUCTION (CREW FOR BUILD, STRIKE)	# MAN DAYS	Estimated	Actual	
43. Set Designer Name:				
44. Carpenters				
45. Grips				
46. Outside Props				
47. Inside Props				
48. Scenics				
49. Electricians				
50. Teamsters				
51. Men for Strike (grips, props, elect., misc.)				
52.				
53.				
54.				
SUB TOTAL D				

man days ....

SET CONSTRUCTION MATERIALS	Estimated	Actual	
55. Props and Set Dressings			
56. Lumber			
57. Paint / Wallpaper			
58. Hardware			
59. Special Effects			
60. Special Outside Construction			
61. Trucking			
62. Messengers / Deliveries			
63.			
SUB TOTAL E			

STUDIO RENTAL & EXPENSES - STAGE:	Estimated	Actual	
64. Rental for Build / Strike (days @ $)			
65. Rental for Pre-Lite Days (days @ $)			
66. Rental for Shoot Days (days @ $)			
67. Rental for Shoot O. T. (Hrs.)			
68. Rental for Build / Strike Days O.T. (Hrs.)			
69. Total Power Charge & Bulbs			
70. Misc. Studio Charges & Service			
71. Meals (Lunches & Dinner for Crew and Talent)			
72.			
73.			
74.			
75.			
SUB TOTAL F			

PAGE 3

LOCATION EXPENSES	Estimated	Actual	
76. Location Fees			
77. Guards			
78. Car Rentals			
79. Bus Rentals			
80. Camper / Dressing Room Vehicles			
81. Parking, Tolls, & Gas			
82. Trucking			
83. Other Vehicles A /			
84. Other Vehicles B /			
85. Special Crew Equipt. / Clothing			
86. Air Freight / Customs / Excess Baggage			
87. Air Fares: No. of people ( ) x cost per fare ( )			
88. Per Diems: Total No. man days ( ) x amt. per day ( )			
89. Breakfast: No. of man days ( ) x amt. per person ( )			
90. Lunch: No. of man days ( ) x amt. per person ( )			
91. Dinner: No. of man days ( ) x amt. per person ( )			
92. Gratuities, Tips and Misc. Outside Labor			
93. Cabs and other passenger transportation			
94. Limousines (Celebrity Service)			
95.			
96.			
97.			
98.			
99.			
SUB TOTAL G			

EQUIPMENT RENTAL	Estimated	Actual	
100. Camera Rental Type:			
101. Sound Rental			
102. Lighting Rental			
103. Grip / Dolly Rental			
104. Generator Rental			
105. Crane / Cherry Picker Rental			
106. VTR Rental			
107. Production Supplies			
108.			
109.			
SUB TOTAL H			

FILM RAW STOCK DEVELOP AND PRINT	Estimated	Actual	
110. Purchase of Raw Stock: footage amount ( ) x per foot			
111. Developing and Printing: footage amount ( ) x per foot			
112. Studio for Transfer: No. of hours ( )			
113. 16mm or 35mm Mag Stock: No. of hours ( )			
114. Sync/Screen Dailies			
115.			
SUB TOTAL I			

PROPS AND WARDROBE	Estimated	Actual	
116. Location Props			
117. Costume/Wardrobe Rental & Purchase			
118. Animals & Handlers			
119. Wigs, Mustaches / Special Make-Up			
120. Color Correction			
SUB TOTAL J			

PAGE 4

DIRECTOR / CREATIVE FEES:	Estimated	Actual	
121. Prep Days			
122. Travel Days			
123. Shoot Days			
124. Post-production Days			
125.			
SUB TOTAL K			

MISCELLANEOUS COSTS	Estimated	Actual	
126. Total Payroll & P & W Taxes % of total of A, B, D, & K			
127. Air Shipping / Special Carriers			
128. Phones and Cables			
129. Misc. (Petty Cash)			
130. Misc. Trucking & Messengers			
131.			
132.			
133.			
SUB TOTAL L			

TALENT	No.	Rate	Days— Fees	Travel	O.T.	Estimated	No.	Days— Fees	Actual
134. O/C Principals									
135. O/C Principals									
136. O/C Principals									
137. O/C Principals									
138. O/C Principals									
139.									
140.									
141.									
142. General Extras									
143. General Extras									
144. General Extras									
145.									
146.									
147.									
148. Hand Model									
149. Voice Over									
150. Fitting Fees									
151. Audition Fees: No. of talent ( ) x Amount ( )									
152. SUB-TOTAL									
153. Payroll & P & W Taxes									
154. Wardrobe Allowance: No. of talent ( ) x No. of garments ( ) x fee per garment ( ).									
155. Agents' Commissions									
156. SUB-TOTAL									
157. Other									
158. Handling Fee (____ %)									
SUB TOTAL M									

TALENT EXPENSES	Estimated		Actual
159. Per diem: No. of man days ( ) x amount per day ( )			
160. Air fare: No. of people ( ) x amount per fare ( )			
161. Cabs and other transportation			
162.			
163.			
164.			
SUB TOTAL N			

PAGE 5

EDITORIAL COMPLETION	Estimated	Actual	
165. Editing			
166. Asst. Editor			
167. Coding			
168. Projection			
169. Artwork for supers			
170. Shooting of artwork			
171. Stock footage			
172. Still photographs			
173. Opticals (incl. pre-optical)			
174. Animation			
175. Stock music			
176. Original music			
177. Sound effects			
178. Dubbing studio			
179. Studio for narration - including transfer to mag. No. of hours ( )			
180. Studio for mixing - including transfer to mag. No. of hours ( )			
181. Negative tracks			
182. Answer & corrected prints			
183. Contract items			
184. Film to tape transfer (incl. reprints & masters)			
185. Film to tape transfer - editorial fee			
186.			
187.			
188. Editorial Handling Fee:			
SUB TOTAL O			

VIDEOTAPE PRODUCTION AND COMPLETION	Estimated	Actual	
189. Basic crew (No. of men:)			
190. Additional crew (No. of men:)			
191. Labor overtime			
192.			
193.			
194. VTR/Camera rental			
195. Additional VTR's/Cameras			
196. Equipment overtime			
197. Special equipment (specify)			
198. Special processes (specify)			
199. Trucking			
200. Mobile unit			
201. Stock (rental ☐ purchase ☐ No. of hrs:)			
202. Screening			
203. On-line editing No. VTR hrs:)			
204. Off-line editing (No. of hrs:)			
205. Videotape A/B roll preparation and stock			
206. Audio mix with VT projection			
207. Video air masters			
208. Video printing dupe			
209. 3/4'' videocassette			
210. Tape to fim transfer			
211. Markup			
SUB TOTAL P			

No. of hours in basic day: _____

No. of travel hours: _____

No. of setup/wrap hours: _____

No. of net shoot hours: _____

Crew O.T. rate per hour: _____

Eqpt./stage O.T. rate per hour: _____

Comments:

Bibliography

Bauer, Raymond A., and Greyser, Stephen A., eds. *The A.A.A.A. Study on Consumer Judgment of Advertising*. Boston: Division of Research, Harvard Graduate School of Business Administration, 1968.

Berry, Leonard L. "The Time Buying Consumer." *Journal of Retailing* 55 (1979).

Burgener, Robert D. "New Electronic Media: Present Capabilities." Edited by Karen Burns. *Direct Response Broadcast and New Electronic Media*. New York: Direct Mail/Marketing Association, Inc., 1980.

Burns, Karen, ed. *Direct Response Broadcast and New Electronic Media*. New York: Direct Mail/Marketing Association, Inc., 1980.

Cable Ad Associates. Press kit. Washington, D.C., 1980.

Caples, John. "How to Test TV Commercials Through Direct Response." *Direct Marketing* (September 1977), pp. 62–63, 83.

Chaffee, Stephen; Comstock, George; Katzman, Nathan; McCombs, Maxwell; and Roberts, Donald. *Television and Human Behavior*. New York: Columbia University Press, 1978.

Davis, Errol. "Telephone Marketing: The IN-WATS Revolution." *Direct Mail/Marketing Manual*. New York: Direct Mail/Marketing Association, Inc., 1979.

Direct Mail/Marketing Association, Inc. *DM/MA Fact Book on Direct Response Marketing*. New York: Direct Mail/Marketing Association, Inc. 1980.

Ellentuck, Shan. "Broadcast—The Sound of Profit for the Direct Marketer." *Direct Mail/Marketing Manual*. New York: Direct Mail/Marketing Association, Inc., 1979.

Elliot, William Y. *Television's Impact on American Culture*. East Lansing, MI: Michigan State University Press, 1956.

Gillett, Peter L. "In-Home Shoppers: An Overview." *Journal of Marketing* (October 1976), pp. 81–87.

Head, Sidney, ed. *Broadcasting in America*. 3d ed. Boston: Houghton Mifflin, 1976.

Hill, Doug. "The Information Revolution Is Coming." *Panorama* 1, no. 2 (March 1980), pp. 70–75.

Information Provider Services. *Key Facts on Prestel*. London.

Knowlton, Thomas. "Selecting the Media Mix." *Direct Mail/Marketing Manual*. New York: Direct Mail/Marketing Association, Inc., 1979.

Kobs, Jim. *Profitable Direct Marketing*. Chicago: Crain Books, 1979.

Levy, Sy; Lewis, Barbara; and Lynaugh, George. "TV Support Can Increase Response by 50% or More." *Direct Marketing*.

Lewis, Barbara. "Broadcast Planning Decisions." Edited by Karen Burns. *Direct Response Broadcast and New Electronic Media*. New York: Direct Mail/Marketing Association, Inc., 1980.

MacLachlan, James, and LaBarbara, Priscilla. "Time-Compressed TV Commercials." *Journal of Advertising Research* (August 1978).

Martin, James. *Future Developments in Telecommunications*. Englewood Cliffs, NJ: Prentice-Hall, 1977.

National Broadcasting Corporation. *Broadcasting: The Next Ten Years*. New York: 1977.

A.C. Nielsen Company. *1979 Nielsen Report on Television*. Northbrook, IL: 1979.

Pearce, Carol A. "Pre-Prod'n Safeguard: Testmakers Coming on Strong." *Backstage* (August 3, 1979), pp. 1, 18–19.

Reynolds, Fred D.; Martin, Warren S.; and Martin, Wendy K. "Media Habits of In-Home Buyers." *Journal of Advertising* 16 (1977), pp. 31–35.

Roper, Burns W. *Changing Public Attitudes Toward Television and Other Mass Media: 1959–1976.* New York: Television Information Office, 1979.

———. *Public Perceptions of Television and Other Mass Media: A Twenty-Year Review 1959–1978.* A Report by the Proper Organization. New York: Television Information Office, 1979.

Rosenberg, Bernard, and White, David Manning, eds. *Mass Culture: The Popular Arts in America.* Glencoe, IL: The Free Press, 1957.

Rosenberg, Larry J., and Hirschman, Elizabeth C. "Retailing Without Stores." *Harvard Business Review* (July/August 1980), pp. 103–110.

Rosenthal, Edmond M. "Testing Commercials." *Television/Radio Age* 25 (1978), pp. 25–28, 52–54.

Schwartz, Larry. "WATS Happening: 800 Numbers Open Up a New Line of Communication for Marketers." *Marketing Communications* (March/April 1977), pp. 40–47.

Stern, Edward. *The Direct Marketing Market Place.* Hilary House Publishers, Inc., 1980.

Stone, Robert. *Successful Direct Marketing Methods.* 2d ed. Chicago: Crain Books, 1979.

"Techniques of Testing TV Commercial Multiply; Creative People Adapt to Them." *Television/Radio Age* 26, no. 7 (November 6, 1978), pp. 30–32, 73–80.

Warner Communications. QUBE Press Kit.

Waters, Harry F., and Marbach, William D. "TV of Tomorrow." *Newsweek* (July 3, 1978), pp. 62–74.

Index